Joseph H. Lupton

Archbishop Wake and the Project of Union (1717-1720) between the Gallican and Anglican Churches by Joseph H. Lupton

Joseph H. Lupton

Archbishop Wake and the Project of Union (1717-1720) between the Gallican and Anglican Churches by Joseph H. Lupton

ISBN/EAN: 9783743343481

Manufactured in Europe, USA, Canada, Australia, Japa

Cover: Foto ©ninafisch / pixelio.de

Manufactured and distributed by brebook publishing software (www.brebook.com)

Joseph H. Lupton

Archbishop Wake and the Project of Union (1717-1720) between the Gallican and Anglican Churches by Joseph H. Lupton

ARCHBISHOP WAKE

AND THE

PROJECT OF UNION

(1717—1720)

BETWEEN THE

GALLICAN AND ANGLICAN CHURCHES.

BY

J[oseph] H. LUPTON, B.D.,

Surmaster of St. Paul's School, and Preacher of Gray's Inn; formerly Fellow of St. John's College, Cambridge.

LONDON:
GEORGE BELL AND SONS, YORK ST. COVENT GARDEN.
CAMBRIDGE: DEIGHTON, BELL AND CO.
1896.

CHISWICK PRESS:—CHARLES WHITTINGHAM AND CO.
TOOKS COURT, CHANCERY LANE, LONDON.

TO
THE MASTERS OF THE BENCH
OF THE HONOURABLE SOCIETY OF GRAY'S INN
THIS DISSERTATION,
WRITTEN FOR A DEGREE SOUGHT AT THEIR DESIRE,
IS MOST RESPECTFULLY DEDICATED.

PREFACE.

IN choosing the subject for a Dissertation required by the statutes of the University of Cambridge, I was attracted to the present one from several causes. As a former Preacher of Gray's Inn, the life and writings of Archbishop Wake had a natural interest for me. Moreover, the frequent discussion, during the past year, of proposals for reunion among separated bodies of Christians tended to recall a period of Wake's life, when his thoughts were much occupied by similar proposals.

It seemed, accordingly, that it might not be useless or inappropriate to relate, in fuller detail than had hitherto been done, a project in which he was once engaged for the reunion of two national Churches. The fact that the scheme to outward appearance proved abortive does not deprive it of its value. The correspondence between two such representative men as an Archbishop of Canterbury and one of the most learned jurists of France, cannot but be instructive. We may at least gain from it a clearer conception of the difficulties that must beset us, when we attempt to reach an end, in itself confessedly good, but towards which the road has not yet been sufficiently levelled and prepared.

The published works of Dr. Wake, like those of his great correspondent Du Pin, afford ample evidence of his learning and industry. But our admiration of these qualities is increased when we survey what he has left unpublished. We marvel how one immersed in public business could have found time to keep up an unceasing correspondence with foreign Churches, and with learned persons in every country of Europe. The manuscripts bequeathed by him to the Library of his old College of Christ Church, Oxford, including books with his annotations in the margin, amount to fully one hundred volumes. And many of these are bulky folios and quartos, filled with letters addressed to him, and with the carefully-prepared drafts of his own replies, in Latin, French, and English.

For permission to transcribe from these manuscript treasures (a permission most courteously conveyed to me by the Rev. T. Vere Bayne, Keeper of the University Archives) I am indebted to the Wake trustees. Several unpublished letters have also been gained from a manuscript formerly in the possession of the Beauvoir family, now numbered " Additional, 22,880" in the Library of the British Museum.

Part of the correspondence here printed was used by Dr. Maclaine for an Appendix to the last volume of his translation of Mosheim's *History*. Wherever I have reproduced any of these letters, I have been careful to give the reference to his work. He appears to have obtained the papers from the Rev. Osmund Beauvoir, a son of Wake's correspondent in Paris; but what has since become of them I have not been able to learn. Short extracts from the letters are also found in two other well-known works,—the *Eirenicon* of Dr. Pusey, and the *History of the Church of France* of the Rev. W. H. Jervis, with its supplementary volume, *The Gallican Church and the Revolution*. To this excellent history I have been much indebted, in writing the two preliminary chapters, which it seemed desirable to prefix as as introduction to the correspondence itself. Scarcely less useful has been the *La France et Rome* of M. Albert le Roy, with its copious extracts from the Jansenist archives at Amersfoort. The older authorities, Pithou, Dupuy, and others, have of course not been neglected.

In a concluding chapter I have tried to indicate briefly how some of the great landmarks of the controversy have shifted their bearings during the century and three-quarters that have elapsed since Wake laid down his pen. But for the fear of unduly enlarging my subject, I should have been tempted to extend the inquiry in the opposite direction as well, by discussing the possibility of a closer union between the Churches of England and France, as it presented itself to the minds of Francis I. and Henry VIII. about the year 1527. In that case also the idea was never realized; the scheme of a Western Patriarchate under Wolsey proved visionary; a partial revival of the negotiations in 1546 came to nothing. To some of the more sanguine spirits among us the result of such inquiries may seem disappointing; the method pursued to be out of sympathy with the ardent aspirations we have heard. If such be the case, I can only plead the necessity of caution, of not letting sentiment intrude into the province of fact. In the words of an eminent Bishop of Blois: "La charité a ses droits; mais la vérité n'a-t-elle pas aussi les siens? sur lesquels jamais on ne doit transiger."

J. H. L.

ST. PAUL'S SCHOOL,
Michaelmas, 1895.

AUTHORITIES.

To avoid repetition, the full titles are here given of some of the authorities most frequently cited in the notes.

Wake Corresp.—The manuscript Letters and Papers of Archbishop Wake in the Library of Christ Church, Oxford. The Roman numerals are those by which the volumes are denoted in Kitchin's catalogue.

Beauvoir Corresp.—A thin volume of manuscript letters, chiefly to or from the Rev. W. Beauvoir, numbered 22,880 in the "Additional MSS." in the British Museum.

Projet d'Union.—A little work, in 12mo, published in 1864 by the Anglo-Continental Society, in French, with the title: *D'un Projet d'Union entre les Églises Gallicane et Anglicane. Correspondance entre Wake, archevêque de Cantorbéri et Dupin, Docteur de Sorbonne.* It contains a French translation of most of the letters given by Maclaine, but does not say whence they are taken.

Maclaine.—The sixth volume of Dr. Archibald Maclaine's translation of Mosheim's *Ecclesiastical History*, ed. 1811. The letters are in Appendix IV.

Lafiteau.—*Histoire de la Constitution* 'Unigenitus,' par Messire Pierre-François Lafiteau, évêque de Sisteron. 2 tom., à Liège, 1738.

Guettée.—*Histoire de l'Église de France, sur les documents originaux et authentiques*, par l'abbé Guettée. Tomes xi., xii., à Paris, 1855.

Jervis, i., ii.—*A History of the Church of France, from the Concordat of Bologna,* A.D. 1516, *to the Revolution*, by the Rev. W. Henley Jervis, M.A., Prebendary of Heytesbury. 2 vols. Lond. 1872.

Jervis, iii.—*The Gallican Church and the Revolution*, a sequel to the preceding, by the same. London, 1882.

Le Roy.—*La France et Rome, de 1700 à 1715: Histoire diplomatique de la Bulle 'Unigenitus' jusqu' à la mort de Louis XIV.*, par Albert Le Roy, à Paris, 1892.

CONTENTS.

CHAPTER I.
ON GALLICANISM.

National Characteristics of Churches—How far in accordance with the spirit of Christianity — Principle of Centralization—The enemy of national independence—Conflict between the two principles—The former encouraged under Louis XIV.—Historical Sketch of Gallicanism—Louis IX.—The Concordat—Schism in the Papacy—Council of Pisa—*Droit de Régale*—Influence of Bossuet—Articles of 1682—Compared with those of 1663—Arbitrary conduct of Louis XIV. 1

CHAPTER II.
STATE OF THE FRENCH CHURCH AT THE TIME OF THE PROJECT.

Events tending to increase the influence of the Papacy—Fénelon and the Quietists—The *Réflexions morales*—Character of De Noailles—The *Problème ecclésiastique*—The *Cas de Conscience*—The Bull *Vineam Domini*—Its reception—Fate of Port-royal—The Bull *Unigenitus*—Acceptance of it disputed—Assembly of Clergy—Parliament—The Sorbonne—Scheme of a National Council. 19

CHAPTER III.
CORRESPONDENCE BETWEEN ARCHBISHOP WAKE AND OTHERS.

Account of William Wake—The English Chaplaincy at Paris—Position of Du Pin and others—Speech of De Girardin in the Sorbonne—Letters of Beauvoir, De Girardin, Du Pin, Harris, Wake—The *Commonitorium* of Du Pin—His opinion of the Articles of the English Church 44

CHAPTER IV.
THE FRENCH CHURCH IN MODERN TIMES.

State of the French Church at the eve of the Revolution—Effect of the Revolution upon it—The *Constitution Civile du Clergé*—The Concordat—The Bourbon Restoration—The Vatican Council of 1870—Present prospects 118

INDEX 137

ARCHBISHOP WAKE AND THE PROJECT OF UNION BETWEEN THE GALLICAN AND ANGLICAN CHURCHES.

CHAPTER I.

On Gallicanism.

WHEN the ties which bind together a people of the same race exert their force in religious matters, a Christian Church, if founded among that people, will bear characteristics that we call national. In proportion to the strength of those ties, compared with any allegiance that may be demanded of it to an external authority, will be the depth and permanence of the characteristics impressed upon its Church.

It may be granted at the outset that the genius of Christianity is adverse to the continuance within it of distinctions of race or nation. In its all-embracing fold it would include alike Jew and Gentile, Greek and barbarian, bond and free. It was designed, we may freely confess, to apply a corrective to that strongly-marked tendency of the ancient world, which would intrench each state or nation within its own fixed limits. It had to assert the brotherhood of man against the religious exclusiveness of the Jew, the political exclusiveness of the Greek or Roman.

But it does not therefore follow that a national character, impressed upon a nation's Christianity at any given period, would in itself be a wrong thing. Institutions may have their use, may deserve and even demand preservation, though we are conscious that their existence cannot be perpetual. Like sandy cliffs, crumbling before an ever-advancing sea, they are serviceable for a time; and prudent men will endeavour to secure and strengthen them as long as possible.

Older writers loved to see this principle of nationality in religion, of the demarcation of Churches by civil boundaries, foreshadowed in Holy Scripture by the distribution of guests at some great banquet. When King Ahasuerus made a feast for his princes and nobles, for his servants and the people of Shushan, "doubtless," writes Bishop Stillingfleet,[1] "the King did equally respect them all as a body in the feasting of them, and did bestow his entertainment upon them all as considered together; but by reason of the great multitude of them, it was impossible that they should all be feasted together in the same room; and therefore, for more participation of the King's bounty, it was necessary to divide themselves into particular companies, and to associate as many as conveniently could in order to that end. So it is in the Church. Christ in donation of priviledges equally respects the whole Church; but because men cannot all meet together to participate of these priviledges, a more particular distribution was necessary for that end." A like inference, but a more cogent one still, was drawn from the grouping of the multitude by companies, when our Lord fed the five thousand. From all which these writers drew the conception of a National Church, not as something dismembered or incomplete in itself, but as a complete and organic whole, a "national union in one ecclesiastical body in the same community of ecclesiastical government."[2]

If we apply the principles here laid down in general terms to the case of a particular nation—in the present instance, France—we shall understand what is meant by Gallicanism. While admitting that the true theory of a Christendom on earth is that of a body with many members and but one head, it denies that in any earthly head there resides despotic authority over the whole. The government of the Church in

---

[1] *Irenicum*, ed. 1662, p. 155.

[2] *Ib.*, p. 157, quoting Hudson: *Of the Church*, cap. i., § 3. [*The Essence and Unitie of the Church Catholike Visible*, by the Rev. S. Hudson, Lond. 1645. 4to.]

this world is not an absolute, but a limited, monarchy; a monarchy which, in fact, is still so far an aristocracy, that the monarch is rather *primus inter pares* than a lord paramount.[1] This, it must be remembered, is the conception of a universal Church formed by a Gallican, one who recognises the Pope as the visible head of that Church, but denies to him any absolute or autocratic power. It will be observed also that while, in the preceding remarks, we have taken the term "Gallicanism" to denote the application to one particular Church of certain general principles, narrowed down in passing from the genus to the species, French writers themselves choose rather to regard the term as expanding outwards to denote the cognate principles in their wider application. "If the principles of religious liberty," says one of them, "took the name of *gallicanism*, it was because France kept possession of the common rights more successfully than other Catholic countries."[2]

It is obvious that to this theory of a co-ordination and independence, within certain limits, of the National Churches composing Christendom, the natural enemy is the principle of centralization, or, as it is now commonly called, ultramontanism. It is among the nations north of the Alps that, as a rule, the opposition to the claims put forth by the Court of Rome is the strongest. Hence the name, though a clumsy one, may be allowed to stand for the line of policy followed by those who would draw to the south of the Alps the supreme control of the Church throughout the world, and vest it in the Bishop of Rome. The contest between these two spiritual forces has been an almost interminable one, with many fluctuations of success. In the reign of Louis XIV. Gallicanism reached its

[1] "On voulait, parmi nous," says the Abbé Puyol, "que l'état chrétien fût non-seulement distinct, mais encore complétement indépendant de l'Église : on affirmait que la monarchie ecclésiastique était, non pas une monarchie pure, mais une monarchie aristocratique. Cette conception fut désigné du nom de Gallicanisme, parce que l'église gallicane s'y attacha avec une particulière passion."— *Edmond Richer: Étude historique*, 1876, tom. i., p. 6.

[2] *Essais sur la Réforme Catholique*, par Bordas-Demoulin et F. Huet, 1856, p. 217.

zenith. It is now, some think, at its lowest, practically extinct; except that, as others believe, principles founded in right, though dormant for a while, never can be extinguished. At any rate, the language used by the spokesmen of the two parties shows the feud to be irreconcileable, and proves how idle is the boast of unity among those, whose favourite argument against Protestants is the diversity of their religious opinions. A Cardinal Archbishop of Paris suspended the licenses of many Jesuits in his province, and inhibited them from administering the sacraments, regarding them "as in rebellion against the Gospel and the Fathers of the Church."[1] The Jesuits, it need not be said, were the foremost champions of the ultramontane cause. "The whole design of the Roman Court," says another Cardinal,[2] writing during the pontificate of Clement XI., "has ever been, and still is, to strive to increase its power, and to trample, as much as possible, on our liberties and customs."

Contrast with this the language used by an organ of modern ultramontanism. "Those who were called Gallicans have been condemned as heretics, and none except those formerly called Ultramontanes can now be reckoned as Catholics." And again: "They (the Gallicans) are as much aliens from the Church or commonwealth of Christ as are Arians, Lutherans, Calvinists, Anabaptists, Methodists, Spiritists, or Devil-worshippers. It is a great mistake to regard Gallicans and Ultramontanes as two parties existing in the Church. Only Ultramontanism is Catholic."[3]

The study of such discordant opinions can never be pleasant, but it may be useful, as showing the justification there was for the *projet d'union* about to be described. In the eyes of the Jesuit writer Lafiteau, that project was only an "abominable complot." So it would have been, if the Gallican Church

---

[1] Le Roy, 506, quoting State Papers.
[2] Cardinal de Janson. *Ib.*, p. 171.
[3] *Brownson's Quarterly Review* (New York), 1874, p. 313. A little less intemperate in its language, but still to the same general effect, is an article in *The Catholic World* (New York), vol. x., pp. 527-541.

in those days had been united in itself, and in perfect accord with a mother Church which was, as it professed to be, the depositary of all Christian truth. But if the real state of things was more like civil war than unbroken peace,[1] the aspect of the case is altered. An intermediary in the negotiations may then be rather compared to a Major André, who, though hanged as a spy on one side of the Atlantic, has a monument in Westminster Abbey erected to him on the other.

Before we come to the *projet* itself, it may be well to trace briefly the growth and development in France of the principles known as Gallicanism, and after that to notice in what posture affairs were in the French Church, at the time when Archbishop Wake began to take part in them.

To reach the source of Gallicanism, if what has been said before is true, we should have to go to the very origin of Christian life in France. So remote an exploration is fortunately not needful for our present subject. It will suffice if we touch the stream of history at a point just seven hundred years above the opening of the Vatican Council. None will deny to St. Louis the title of Catholic. Yet by the well-known "Pragmatic Sanction" of 1269 he obtained for his country privileges now said to be subversive of Catholicism: (1) "The right of election in cathedral and other ecclesiastical institutions was secured from Papal influence. (2) The patronage of benefices and other clerical offices was made subject to the common law (*droit commun*), by which was meant the old Catholic ground-principle of the whole Church. (3) The prelates, and so before all the bishops, were to hold their rights undiminished. (4) Only in the most extreme cases, and not without permission of the Church and the King, was money to be taken out of France by the Pope."[2]

[1] "On se demande sans cesse: 'Comment la France, en temps de conflit avec la Papauté, a-t-elle échappé au schisme définitif?'.... Par une bénédiction spéciale de la Providence."—L'abbé Puyol, as before, i. p. 9.

[2] See an article by Dr. J. A. Dorner, of Berlin, in the *Contemporary Review*, July, 1871, p. 595. Bossuet, after quoting the words of the *Pragmatique*, exclaims: "Ne demandez plus ce que c'est que les

The importance of the rights thus established is soon perceived. They affirmed the principle that bishops, whether of the French or any other Church, are not mere delegates of the Pope, but have an authority co-ordinate with his own. It is not his to choose or nominate them. They may accept at his hands confirmation or investiture when nominated; but they remain officers of the National Church to which they belong. By the last clause a check was put on the interference of the Popes in the secular administration of a State.

Early in the next century, the battle was fought out over again between Philip le Bel and Pope Boniface VIII. The quarrel had arisen over an attempt made by the French king to tax the clergy, as well as laity, of his realm. In this he was technically in the wrong; but the Pope, by the extravagance of his demands, put himself equally in the wrong. It was thus a fair trial of strength between two well-matched powers, and the lay potentate triumphed. "On the 10th of April, 1302, the King held a Grand Parliament, or meeting of the three estates of the kingdom, in the Cathedral of Notre Dame, and frankly asked the advice of his people in the critical state of his relations with the Holy See. Was it their opinion that the sovereign was subject to the Bishop of Rome, not only in spirituals, but as to the conduct of his temporal government? Was the kingdom of France an independent Monarchy, or was it held in feudal vassalage from the Pope? To these questions the nobles and the deputies of the commons responded, with unanimous enthusiasm, that the crown was held of God alone, and that they were ready to sacrifice both property and life, rather than submit to the outrageous usurpations of Pope Boniface, even if the King himself were not disposed to withstand them."[1] The clergy wavered, but ultimately their representatives sided with the rest, after they had written to warn the Holy See of the danger of a schism

---

libertés de l'Église gallicane. Les voilà toutes dans ces précieuses paroles de l'ordonnance de Saint-Louis."—*Sermon prêché à l'ouverture*, etc., 1681 (*Œuvres*, 1816, xv. 534).

[1] Jervis, i. 63.

between France and Rome. This did not end the strife, which only ceased, for a time, with the melancholy death of Boniface in October of the following year. But it is enough for our present purpose, as showing the continuance, in full vigour, of the spirit of Gallicanism in France.

The great schism in the Papacy, a century later, served not only to strengthen the Gallican principles in France, but also to diffuse them through other countries. That the supreme governing power of the Church on earth resided in a General Council, not in any individual Pope, was a theory that many had held, but had not seen exemplified in practice. Boniface had ridiculed the notion of a General Council being called without him, or by any other than himself. Whether this ridicule was well-timed was now to be seen. On March 25th, 1409, the Council of Pisa began its sessions. That it deposed both the rival popes, and declared the Holy See vacant, is one of the most familiar matters of history. It should be noticed, however, how large and powerful was the French element in this Council. Cardinal D'Ailly and Chancellor Gerson were its master-spirits. So that, whatever discredit may be attempted to be thrown on its claim to the title of general, the work of the Council may be regarded to a great extent as directed by France; its results a triumph of Gallicanism.

A further advance in the same direction was marked by the Pragmatic Sanction of Bourges. That measure, says Jervis, was a protest "against the crying evils of Mediævalism. It denounced the 'réservations,' 'dévolutions,' 'expectatives,' by means of which the richest benefices of France were often conferred upon unknown foreigners, who never resided among their flocks, and could not speak their language.... It prescribed canonical election, and confirmation by the Metropolitans. It abolished the 'annates.' It regulated the system of appeals to Rome, and enjoined that all ecclesiastical causes should pass through the various gradations of local jurisdiction."[1]

[1] *Gallican Church*, ii. 420. See also Grégoire: *Discours pour l'ouverture*, etc., 1801, p. 9.

This second Pragmatic Sanction was registered by the Parliament of Paris, July 13th, 1439; and thus for a while longer the "liberties" of the Gallican Church continued to be part of the law of the land.

We now approach the time when Gallicanism exposed itself to the reproach, since then so freely poured upon it by its enemies, of being only Erastianism under another name. The suspicious and arbitrary mind of Louis XI. was worked upon to revoke the Sanction, soon after his accession in 1461. For a while the Parliament of Paris treated this revocation as null, and a state of disorder in things ecclesiastical ensued, which lasted through the reigns of Louis XII. and of the martial Pope Julius II. With the accession of Francis I. the contest was resumed on less unequal terms. The young "Roi chevalier" was flushed with the recent victory of Marignano. Leo X. was more anxious for peace than his predecessor had been, and so an agreement was come to in the Concordat of Bologna, August 18th, 1516. By this instrument the provisions of the Pragmatic Sanction of Bourges were formally repealed. The right of nomination to bishoprics and other "consistorial benefices" was transferred from the capitular bodies to the Crown. "The King was to present, within six months after the vacancy, a doctor or licentiate in divinity to the Pope, who was thereupon to confirm the appointment and confer canonical institution."[1] By the designed omission of any clause forbidding it, the claim of the Papacy to the annates was allowed to be revived.

Throughout the French nation a strenuous opposition was raised to the new enactments, and especially to the resuscitated demand for annates. The Parliament of Paris, the magistrates, the doctors of the Sorbonne, were united in their condemnation of it. A Bull of Leo and a Royal Message from Francis were alike powerless to lay the storm. In deference to the King's mandate, Parliament did at last accept and register the Concordat, March 22nd, 1517; but this was done with an ill grace, while the great body of the

[1] Jervis, i. 106.

clergy still continued their protest. At Melun, in 1579, and again at the synod held in 1588, they renewed their remonstrances. They felt that the change from nomination by the Chapter to nomination by the Crown was not only an infringement of the ancient rights of the Church, but was certain also to produce an inferior type of prelates—men who would be courtiers first and bishops afterwards, disqualified for making any stand against the encroachments of the monarchy. Such were those against whom Racine directed his scornful epigram:

> "Un ordre, hier venu de St. Germain,
> Veut qu'on s'assemble: on s'assemble demain.
> Notre Archevêque, et cinquante-deux autres
>   Successeurs des Apôtres,
> S'y trouveront. Or de savoir quel cas
> S'y traitera, c'est encore un mystère.
> C'est seulement chose très-claire
> Que nous avons cinquante-deux Prélats
>   Qui ne resident pas."[1]

The events of the Reformation era did not shake the Gallican Church so deeply as might have been expected. More important in its permanent influence upon it was the birth of that great power which dogged the Reformation like a Nemesis, the order of Ignatius Loyola. These "perturbateurs du repos public," as the Abbé Guettée calls them, were the persistent, relentless enemies of Gallicanism. Its continuance was a standing protest against the one object for which they strove—the subjection of all things to the Pope. To compass its destruction, they ceased not to work upon the minds of the French kings till Louis XIV., on his deathbed, could solemnly call to witness Cardinals Rohan and Bissy, in presence of his confessor, le Père Tellier, that he had acted throughout under their guidance: "C'était à eux de répondre devant Dieu pour lui de tout ce qui s'était fait, de trop ou du trop peu, qu'il y était parfaitement ignorant."[2]

---

[1] *Œuvres*, ed. 1769, tom. v., p. 303.
[2] Le Roy, p. 690, on the authority of Saint-Simon: *Mémoires*, viii. 67. The king's words, according to Dorsanne (*ib.*), were: "Si

In spite, however, of the control exercised by Le Tellier, and others of his order, over the mind of Louis XIV., the force of circumstances threw him, towards the latter part of his long reign, into antagonism with the Pope, and thus identified more closely the cause of the Gallican Church with the Monarchy. The contest arose about the exercise of the *droit de régale;* a subject which may need a few words of explanation.

The right in question was one of great antiquity in France, and seems to have had its origin in the feudal system. By virtue of it, the King claimed the reversion to himself of the temporalities of vacant sees, just as, on the decease of a feudal tenant, the land he had held reverted to the seigneur.[1] But more than that. As the temporalities and the spiritual functions both appertained to the occupant of the see, he who had assumed charge of the one, *sede vacante*, was bound to provide for the fulfilment of the other. Hence, according to one theory, the King might lawfully exercise the ecclesiastical patronage of the bishopric, the temporalities of which he had for the time resumed. Some Churches, chiefly in the south of France, claimed to be exempt from this *droit de régale* and a determined opposition had been offered to attempts to enforce it.

Things were in this state when Louis XIV. issued his well-known Declaration, February 10th, 1673, "alleging that the *droit de régale* belonged to him, in all the archbishoprics and bishoprics throughout the kingdom, with the exception of those which were exempt *à titre onéreux;* that is, in virtue of distinct cessions or exchanges formerly effected at their cost, and to the advantage of the Crown."[2] What made this Declaration more galling was that it was retrospective in its effects. Bishops of dioceses hitherto considered exempt were required to submit to certain forms, to obtain restitution of

vous m'avez trompé, vous êtes bien coupables, car je ne cherche que le bien de l'église."

[1] This is the view taken by Jervis, ii. 24.
[2] Jervis, ii. 25.

their temporalities, as though they had before held them without any lawful title. Most complied; but two out of the number—Nicolas Pavillon, Bishop of Alet, and François de Caulet, Bishop of Pamiers—absolutely refused. On the death of the former of these, in 1677, the resistance to the King's mandate was kept up with undiminished fervour by the Bishop of Pamiers. The Pope of that day, Innocent XI., was also unflinching in support of the Bishop; while the Jesuits, influenced, it is said, by motives of private enmity to De Caulet and his late colleague,[1] threw the weight of their support on the side of the King. A curious re-arrangement of parties was thus for a time formed, and complications resulted, from which there seemed no way of escape but by a General Assembly of the Clergy. A committee of three archbishops and three bishops was appointed to draw up a report on the subject; and in accordance with their recommendation such a General Assembly was called for October 1st, 1681.[2]

At this gathering there was present one destined to exercise a powerful influence on the fortunes of Gallicanism, and whose memory was to be inseparably associated with it. Jacques Bénigne Bossuet, late Bishop of Condom, had just been translated to the see of Meaux,[3] and he was the one now chosen to preach the sermon at the formal opening of the Assembly. For this responsible task Bossuet made the most careful preparation. He submitted his sermon before delivery to the Archbishops of Paris and Rheims, and also to Cardinal d'Estrées, a chargé d'affaires at Rome. It was worthy of the occasion. Taking his text from Numbers xxiv. 5, *Quam pulchra tabernacula tua, Iacob, et tentoria tua, Israel*, he enlarged on "the beauty and glory of the Church Catholic." The love of peace, which is disclosed in his correspondence,

---

[1] Guettée, xi. 38.

[2] The formal opening of the Assembly, according to Guettée, was on Oct. 30th. The Mass of the Holy Ghost, at which Bousset was the preacher, was on Nov. 9th.

[3] He was nominated May 2nd, 1681. Innocent XI. sent him the Bull of Investiture in October of the same year.

animated him in this eloquent discourse. For the attainment of that peace he saw no hope but in mutual concessions of the two powers, the kingly and the papal. Hence he pleaded with equal impressiveness for "the unity of the Church, of which the Holy See is the centre; and for the tradition of the Church of France, touching episcopal authority and the independence of the temporal power."[1]

The part Bossuet had to play was a difficult one. There is no doubt that he held the principles embodied in the four Declarations to be presently described. But he thought the expression of them at that time was inopportune, and likely to increase the tension of feeling existing between the King and the Pope. Each of these potentates, moreover, had a claim upon his gratitude for many marks of favour. It has been not unnatural to suppose that a letter addressed by the Assembly to the Pope, in January, 1682, explaining and defending the line they had taken in the matter of the *régale*, was drawn up by Bossuet. But he himself attributed it to Le Tellier, Archbishop of Rheims.[2] The letter was temperate and respectful in its language. But unfortunately Innocent XI. deferred his reply to it, and in the interval the Assembly had proceeded to its great work of framing the Declarations. The Pope's impetuous temper was not rendered more placable by this. He reproached the assembled bishops in his Brief of April 11th with cowardice and servility. If they had not fallen, it was because they had never stood upright. If they had not been vanquished, it was because they had not fought. Which of them had set himself as a wall to protect the house of their spiritual Israel? The King's ministers had lifted up their voice for the royal prerogatives: they, with a better cause to

---

[1] Guettée, xi. 67. A full analysis of the sermon is in Jervis, ii. 38-43. It was printed, by request of the Assembly, in December, 1681, and published in the beginning of 1682. The Assembly itself is known as that of 1682, because it did not formulate its declarations till March in that year.

[2] This was Charles Maurice Le Tellier, an opponent of the Jesuits, not to be confounded with Michel Le Tellier, confessor to Louis XIV., or with the Chancellor Le Tellier, who died within a month after affixing the great seal to the document revoking the Edict of Nantes.

defend, had been silent, when the honour of Christ was at stake. "Not without a feeling of horror," the Brief went on, "have we read that part of your letter in which you inform us of the abandonment of your rights, and of your transfer of them to the King: as if you were the owners, not the guardians only, of the Churches intrusted to you; as if the very Churches and their spiritual rights could be abandoned to the temporal power by the Bishops, who should rather have submitted to be made bondsmen themselves, than endanger the liberty of the Churches."[1]

Nearly a month before this letter would reach the Assembly —with sufficient space, therefore, to allow of the news of their proceedings reaching Rome, and further exasperating the Pontiff—its members had passed their four famous Declarations. These bear date March 19th, 1682. That Bossuet drew them up is certain. That it was on his recommendation that the Assembly entered on the task at all, is contradicted, not only by what we know of his sentiments, but explicitly by an entry in the journal of his secretary, L'abbé Le Dieu.[2] It is there distinctly stated, on Bossuet's own authority, that the prime mover was M. Colbert, at that time Secretary of State. He represented to the King that the time was propitious for ascertaining the sense of the Church of France on the justice of the Papal claims, which, at a less disturbed season, men might be afraid to raise, for fear of disturbing the existing calm.

The very argument used points to an unsettled state of opinions on Church matters. It was indeed a critical moment in France. The splendour of the French throne, not yet dimmed by losses abroad, must have tended to exalt its strong-willed occupant, as a *præsens divus*, over the remoter majesty of Rome, in the eyes of those prelates, at least, who owed their exaltation to him. The offence given by the tone of Innocent's letter, when it arrived, was in fact so great, that the two powerful Archbishops of Paris and Rheims (De

[1] See the extracts in Guettée, xi. 77.
[2] Under January 19th, 1700. *Ib.*, p. 81 *n.*

Harlai and Le Tellier) "would not have hesitated a moment," we are told, "to take their stand by the King, in a contest with the Pope, even to the extent of creating a schism; while others, like Gilbert de Choiseul, though they would not have made an open breach with Rome, were so aggrieved by what it had done during the last century to lay the yoke of ultramontanism upon them, that they would not have hesitated to raise a barrier against the encroachments of the Papacy, and to enter on a struggle so determined, that a schism might have been the result in this case no less than in the other."[1]

It will thus be seen that the task set before the new Bishop of Meaux, in drawing up the Declarations, was no easy one; and the reader will be prepared to find that they represent, not the high-water mark, so to speak, of Gallicanism in France at that period, but rather the temperate opinions of one who felt bound to maintain the traditional rights and franchises of his country's Church, but yet was none the less anxious to avoid any estrangement from the See of Rome.

The preamble of the Declarations sets forth the fact that there are two opposite parties, one of which "labours to subvert the Gallican decrees and liberties which our ancestors defended with so much zeal, and their foundations which rest upon the sacred canons and the tradition of the Fathers;" while the other, "under the pretext of those liberties, seeks to derogate from the primacy of St. Peter and of the Roman Pontiffs his successors." With a view to remedy such evils, "we, the archbishops and bishops assembled at Paris by the King's orders, representing, together with the other deputies, the Gallican Church, have judged it advisable, after mature deliberation, to determine and declare as follows:[2]

1. "St. Peter and his successors, vicars of Christ, and likewise the Church itself, have received from God power in things

---

[1] Guettée, xi. 79.

[2] The Declarations will be found, in the original Latin, in *Libertés de l'Église Gallicane*, Paris, 1826, p. 12; in a French translation in Guettée, xi. 80, *sqq.*; and in English, in Jervis, ii. 49-51, which is the translation given in the text.

spiritual and pertaining to salvation, but not in things temporal and civil ; inasmuch as the Lord says, *My kingdom is not of this world;* and again, *Render unto Cæsar the things which be Cæsar's, and unto God the things which be God's.* The Apostolic precept also holds : *Let every soul be subject unto the higher powers ; for there is no power but of God ; the powers that be are ordained of God ; whosoever therefore resisteth the power, resisteth the ordinance of God.* Consequently kings and princes are not by the law of God subject to any ecclesiastical power, nor to the keys of the Church, with respect to their temporal government. Their subjects cannot be released from the duty of obeying them, nor absolved from the oath of allegiance ; and this maxim, necessary to public tranquillity, and not less advantageous to the Church than to the State, is to be strictly maintained, as conformable to the word of the Fathers, and the example of the Saints.

2. "The plenitude of power in things spiritual, which resides in the Apostolic See and the successors of St. Peter, is such that at the same time the decrees of the Œcumenical Council of Constance, in its fourth and fifth sessions, approved as they are by the Holy See and the practice of the whole Church, remain in full force and perpetual obligation ; and the Gallican Church does not approve the opinion of those who would depreciate the said decrees as being of doubtful authority, insufficiently approved, or restricted in their application to a time of schism.

3. "Hence the exercise of the Apostolic authority must be regulated by the canons enacted by the Spirit of God, and consecrated by the reverence of the whole world. The ancient rules, customs, and institutions, received by the realm and Church of France, remain likewise inviolable ; and it is for the honour and glory of the Apostolic See that such enactments, confirmed by the consent of the said See and of the Churches, should be observed without deviation.

4. "The Pope has the principal place in deciding questions of faith, and his decrees extend to every church and all

churches; but nevertheless his judgment is not irreversible until confirmed by the consent of the Church."

"These articles," it was added, "expressing truths which we have received from our fathers, we have determined to transmit to all the Churches of France, and to the bishops appointed by the Holy Ghost to preside over them, in order that we may all speak the same thing, and concur in the same doctrine."

The studied moderation and conciliatory tone in which these articles were framed becomes more apparent when they are placed side by side with an earlier code, framed in 1663, which it had even been the wish of Coquelin, Chancellor of Notre Dame, to issue afresh on the present occasion, as an adequate statement of the Gallican tenets. These articles of 1663, it should be premised, had been drawn up by the Theological Faculty of the University of Paris, at the request of Louis XIV., with a view to checking the spread of ultramontane teaching, then fostered by the Queen Mother, Marie de Médici, and Cardinals Du Perron and Mazarin. They were as follows:[1]

1. "It is not the doctrine of the Faculty that the Pope hath any authority over the temporal power of the King: on the contrary, it hath always opposed even them who assign to him an indirect authority alone.

2. "It is the doctrine of the Faculty that the King owneth not and hath not any superior in temporal things save God alone. This is its ancient doctrine, from which it will never depart.

3. "It is the doctrine of the said Faculty that the King's subjects do owe him fidelity and obedience in such wise that they cannot be dispensed from it, under any pretence soever.

4. "The said Faculty approveth not, nor hath ever approved any propositions contrary to the authority of the King, or the

---

[1] Guettée, xi. 82, quoting Du Pin: *Histoire Ecclésiastique du xviie Siècle*, tom. ii.

true liberties of the Gallican Church, and the canons received in the realm: for example, that the Pope hath power to depose bishops, contrary to the disposal of the said canons.

5. "It is not the doctrine of the Faculty that the Pope is above a General Council.

6. "It is not the doctrine or a dogma [1] of the Faculty that the Pope is infallible, when no consent of the Church intervenes."

But, notwithstanding the more precise and scholastic form of the earlier articles, it is evident that on two most important points they are at one with the later Declarations: that is, on the independence of the temporal power, and the non-residence of infallibility in the Pope.

After the formal adoption of the four Declarations on the 19th of March, the heads of the Commission repaired to St. Germain's, and presented their report to the King. The royal edict, issued in accordance with it, was registered by Parliament on the 23rd, and became part of the law of the land. In some quarters a violent opposition was raised. Bossuet was assailed by a number of ultramontane writers; among whom Roccaberti, Archbishop of Valencia, was conspicuous for his bitterness.[2] These invectives drew from him a work of lasting value, his *Defensio Declarationis Cleri Gallicani*, on which he was working at intervals till his death, but which did not see the light till 1730, nor, in its complete form, till 1745.[3]

---

[1] That is, "it neither is, nor hath been held:" οὔτε δοκεῖ οὔτε δέδοκται.

[2] Roccaberti's work, *De Pontificia Potestate*, was in three folio volumes; but its title was modest compared with that of a treatise by the Marquis Ceroli de Carreto: *Antigraphum ad cleri Gallicani de ecclesiastica potestate declarationem, Optimo, maximo, summoque Pontifici, Christi Vicario, Innocentio XI., urbis et orbis Domino, Cælorum, Terrarum, Inferorumque Janitori unico, fideique oraculo infallibili, humiliter dicat, consecrat, præsentat Nicolaus Ceroli ex Marchionibus de Carreto.*

[3] Owing to this postponement of publication, and to the difference between the editions of 1730 and 1745, attempts have been made to disprove the genuineness of the work. But the Abbé Le Dieu has shown that Bossuet was engaged upon it to the time of his death in 1704. Dr. J. A. Dorner, writing in the *Contemporary Review*, vol. xvii., p. 604, assumes that Bossuet "was not at liberty to publish his defence of the Gallican

One indirect result of the Convention of 1682, interesting as regards our present purpose, was that an effort was made to win back the affections of English and other Protestants. It was felt that one insurmountable barrier to the reunion of foreign Protestants with the See of Rome was the teaching of such writers as Dubois and Ceroli de Carreto.[1] If they were the true and legitimate exponents of the Catholic doctrine, then the monstrous proposition that princes might be deposed at the will of the Pope, and their lives be placed at the mercy of their subjects, would have to be accepted by those seeking reunion. To the fierce reaction against such teaching was ascribed, by no less thoughtful a man than Antoine Arnauld, the cruel treatment experienced by Catholics in Protestant countries; as an example of which was adduced the execution of Strafford in this country. Accordingly, when the work of the Declarations of 1682 was finished, the Assembly set itself to compose a circular letter to Protestants in general, holding out inducements to them to return to the bosom of the Church, and condemning the moral teaching of the Casuists.[2] Whether anything would have come of these endeavours, it is impossible to say. But Louis soon put a stop to them by dissolving the Assembly: at whose instigation, may be easily conjectured.

As we pause at this period in the history of the Gallican Church, and try to estimate its gains and losses, we have to guard against the tendency to be carried away by its imposing aspect, and by the greatness of the names that still adorned it. It is evident that the result of recent conflicts had been, not so much to extend or consolidate its liberties, as to give it a change of masters. What the Pope had surrendered, the King had gained. The enforcement more widely than ever of the rights of the *Regalia* tended to produce a subservient episcopate, a race of courtier prelates, who, as the century went on, proved of little avail to stem the growing tide of revolution.

clergy during the lifetime of Louis." The identical manuscript of the work, which Bossuet bequeathed to his nephew, afterwards Bishop of Troyes, was discovered, in 1812, in the Royal Library at Paris.

[1] See the last note but one.
[2] Guettée, xi. 87.

CHAPTER II.

State of the French Church at the time of the Project.

AFTER this brief survey of what is known as Gallicanism, we must proceed to notice the position of affairs in the French Church during the years immediately preceding the Project of Union. Anything like a full view of so wide a field will be, of course, impossible. Our chief object must be to ascertain what causes of dissatisfaction with Church doctrines or Church government were to be found, which might account, if only in some measure, for the advances made toward such a union.

One of the first events of importance in the religious history of France, after the transactions of the Assembly of 1682, was of a nature to enhance the dignity of the See of Rome, and in so far to arrest the growth of any desire to fraternize with Churches not in communion with it. This was the rise of Quietism, and the final submission to the Papal decrees of Fénelon, its most illustrious convert. That the appeal for final decision in the dispute had to be carried, or at any rate was carried, to Rome, was a circumstance which markedly strengthened the cause of Papal supremacy, as against Gallican independence.

The mystic, or contemplative, form of piety, which on one side developed into the excesses of a Molinos or a Lacombe, had from the earliest times found a congenial home in France. The arch-mystagogue, Dionysius Pseudo-Areopagita, was by many identified with the patron saint of France. It was in that country that the writings of Dionysius found their earliest translators, their ablest exponents: John Scotus Erigena, Hugh and Richard of St. Victor, St François de Sales: names worthy to rank beside Bonaventura, à Kempis, or John Tauler of Strasbourg. But when Madame Guyon, reducing to an absurdity the principles of Molinos, had infected, not merely the impressionable nuns of St. Cyr, but an Archbishop of Cambrai, it was felt by the more rational members of the Church in France that a stand must be made against the spread of such disorders. This led to examinations of Madame Guyon, which need not be related here, and to a direct challenge to Fénelon to acknowledge, or publicly disavow, his approbation of her principles. Bossuet, in his *Instruction sur les états d'oraison*, which occupied him during parts of 1695 and 1696, submitted the doctrines of the Quietists to a searching examination; and, having done this, sent the manuscript of his work to Fénelon for him to subscribe his approval to it. Fénelon, resenting the application, either as being too imperious in its tone, or as involving a desertion of his old friend Madame de Guyon, declined to endorse the work of Bossuet, and, as his best justification, brought out in the beginning of 1697 his *Explication des Maximes des Saints sur la Vie intérieure*. The publication of this work was hastened, by injudicious friends, that it might anticipate the appearance of Bossuet's *Instruction*, which it did by about a month.

Whatever the merits or demerits of the *Maximes*, it was evident that the circumstances of its publication so increased the offence given by the author, that there was little prospect of the work being fairly judged in France. The King, who had no capacity for understanding the Quietist doctrines on their better side, and no personal liking for Fénelon, was further prejudiced against him by the all-powerful Bishop of Meaux. Episcopal conferences showed no indulgence towards the author. And so, not unnaturally, Fénelon resolved to appeal to Rome. He wrote to Innocent XI., and sought permission to go in person, to plead his cause; but this the King refused.[1]

"The Roman Court," in Guettée's words, "eagerly accepted

---

[1] Guettée, xi. 159.

the Archbishop of Cambrai's reference of his cause to it. It was well-pleased on this occasion to be made the final court of appeal in the case of a Bishop, and to have at its feet those who were lately the most active in denying the judicial authority that it claimed as a right."[1] It is no part of our purpose to follow the arguments used on either side in this memorable appeal, or to mark the wearisome delays which attended it in its successive stages. Suffice it to say that on March 12th, 1699, Innocent at length issued a Brief, condemning as erroneous twenty-three propositions from the *Maximes des Saints*. The result was a triumph to the French King and to Bossuet, and this was generally received with favour throughout the kingdom. None the less, the fact of such a decision being asked and delivered at all was a concession to the claims of the Papacy, and in so far a diminution of the liberties of the Church of France. The government tried to break the fall, by directing the metropolitans to summon the bishops of their provinces to debate on the acceptance of the Brief, and thus to show themselves to be assessors of the Pope, not mere followers and servants. The Avocat-Général, d'Aguesseau, used all his eloquence before the assembled Parliament, when the document was finally to be registered, August 14th, 1699, to make it appear that the Gallican liberties had not been invaded; that the Pope, "though the most exalted, was yet not the sole judge of the faith;" that the French bishops had their seats *after* him, but yet *with* him; and that the Brief would be registered with the saving clause: *salva priscorum canonum auctoritate*.[2] A fatal defect had been acknowledged, when theological disputes between Frenchmen could not be decided in France. "Every successive instance of such weakness," says Jervis,[3] "damaged the cause of Gallicanism; and hence we must not be surprised to find that the aggressions upon it became bolder and more offensive, and that, although there was not wanting a firm front of resistance, that resistance was made with

---

[1] Guettée, xi. 160. [2] Jervis, ii. 157. [3] *Ib.*, p. 159.

diminished resources, and with less and less prospect of victory."

The condemnation of the *Maximes* brings us very nearly to the close of the seventeenth century. The succeeding century opens with brilliant prospects lying before the Church in France, but with clouds gathering that soon overcast the sky.

The mischief that threatened lay in the revival, or supposed revival, of Jansenist doctrines. Cornelius Jansen, made Bishop of Ypres in 1636, and dying prematurely of the plague in the following year, was one of those men whose works live after them. His *Augustinus*[1] did not see the light till after his death, being published at Louvain, by the help of friends, in 1640. It was condemned soon after its appearance by a Bull of Urban VIII., *In Eminenti*, but was upheld by Antoine Arnauld in his *De la fréquente Communion*, in 1643. It was from a distinction drawn by the legally-trained intellect of Arnauld, that the terms *de facto* and *de jure* came into vogue in the Jansenist controversy. When the Sorbonne, being divided in their decision on five propositions, alleged to be drawn from Jansen's writings, had allowed the matter to be referred to Rome, Innocent X., by his Bull *Cum Occasione*, in 1653, formally condemned them. The distinction *de facto* and *de jure* was now pressed into the service of the disputants on one side. The Bull had not named Jansen; and it was open to his disciples to assert, that while the Pope might *de jure* condemn the five propositions, they were not *de facto* contained in his writings. The controversy, as all are aware, soon became much more exciting by the intervention of Pascal; and there appeared no prospect of the storm being laid to rest till 1668, when Clement IX. allowed the validity of the distinction. This was regarded as a cessa-

---

[1] *AUGUSTINUS: Doctrina S. Augustini de Humanæ Naturæ sanitate, ægritudine, medicina;* etc. Tom. i. *in quo Hæreses et Mores Pelagii ex S. Augustino recensentur et refutantur.* Tom. ii. *in quo genuina sententia profundissimi Doctoris de auxilio gratiæ . . . proponitur.*

tion of hostilities, and a medal was struck to commemorate the peace.[1]

But within three years a little book was published by Savreux in Paris, which was again to let loose the elements of strife. The book, in its earliest form, was to all appearance a very inoffensive one. It took its rise in a short collection of "Pensées pieuses," made by a Father Jourdain, Superior of the Congregation of the Oratoire in Paris, inserted in a collection of the words of Jesus Christ. M. de Loménie, who had been Secretary of State, but had quitted worldly cares and entered the brotherhood of the Oratory, prevailed on Father Quesnel, newly made director of the institution, to translate these "Pensées" from the Latin, and add to them a preface. When some few additions had been further made, the whole was published, in 1671, under the title: *Abrégé de la morale de l'Évangile, ou pensées chrétiennes sur le texte des quatre évangelistes, pour en rendre la lecture et la méditation plus facile à ceux qui commencent à s'y appliquer.*[2]

The author, or rather editor, of it, was a disciple of Arnauld. It may not be improper to give a few particulars of a life which St. Beuve calls "la préface indispensable et l'ouverture de ce jansénisme du xviiie siècle."

Pasquier Quesnel came, it is said, of Scotch extraction. His father, Jacques, was a bookseller; his mother was Geneviève Paulery.[3] Before entering the Oratory, which he did in 1657, he had studied for seven years in the Jesuit College of Clermont, Paris. He was ordained priest in 1659, at the age of twenty-six. The confidence his Society felt in him was shown, as mentioned above, by his being appointed Director of the Congregation in Paris.

Such was the author, and so unpretending the book, issued at first with the approval of the excellent Félix Vialart, Bishop of Châlons, from which such troubles were to arise.

---

[1] See the article "Jansenists" in Blunt's *Dictionary of Sects, Heresies*, etc., 1874.
[2] Le Roy, pp. 4, 5.
[3] *Ib.*, p. 6 *n.*, quoting an entry in the Archives of the Oratory at Paris.

As if to make the palinode more marked, the Jesuit confessor of the King, Père la Chaise, is said by Saint-Simon[1] to have kept the *Réflexions* always on his table, as "an admirable mine of learning and piety;" and even Pope Clement himself, who ultimately condemned the work, is said to have exclaimed, after reading it, that "there was no one in Rome capable of such writing."

It is a complicated story, how so innocent-looking an off-spring of the press came to raise the storm it did. One cause is doubtless to be found in the growth and enlargement of the work itself. By 1693 it filled four octavo volumes. But even in that form it bore the endorsement of De Noailles, who had succeeded Vialart in the see of Châlons. During the interval, however, its author had become more and more a marked man. In 1684 he had left the Oratory, owing to a refusal to subscribe some form condemnatory of Jansenism, and had soon afterwards retired to Holland, where he attached himself devotedly to Antoine Arnauld. On the death, August 8th, 1694, of that "simple-hearted child of the Church," as Racine calls him,[2] Quesnel became the acknowledged head of the party that had looked to Arnauld as its leader. Hence, by the time that a new edition, following that of 1693, was in contemplation, prejudices had been raised both against the author and his work, which made episcopal approval of the *Réflexions* more difficult.

Moreover, in the archbishopric of Paris a change was made, just about this time, which involved important consequences. In August, 1695, just a year after Arnauld, De Harlai died at the age of seventy. It was expected that Bossuet would be chosen to succeed him,[3] but the King was fastidious on the

---

[1] *Mémoires*, v. 412, quoted by Le Roy, p. 12 *n*. But Le Roy admits that these may be but the *commérages* of history.

[2] "Sublime en ses écrits, doux et simple de cœur,

* * * * * *

L'Église n'eut jamais, même en ses premiers temps,
De plus zélé vengeur ni d'enfant plus docile."

[3] Jervis, ii. 89.

score of high birth, and nominated Louis Antoine, brother of the Duc de Noailles. De Noailles had been consecrated Bishop of Cahors in 1680; but in half a year's time had been translated to Châlons-sur-Marne, where he succeeded Vialart. His elevation to the arch-diocese of Paris raised the hopes of the Jansenists, whose opinions De Noailles had always been supposed to regard with indulgence.

Unfortunately, the new archbishop was a man in whom good intentions were unsupported by strength of will. He was well-meaning, but irresolute; weak, where he should have stood firm; obstinate, when it would have been wiser to yield in time. His wavering, undecided character was well caught by one of the versifiers of the day:

> "Et Noailles jusques au bout
> Sera semblable à la pendule,
> Qui vient, qui revient et recule."

He was, in fact, styled "notre reculante Eminence."[1] More than once, the helm of the Church of France was absolutely in his grasp, but he had not the nerve to steer, and was drifted with the current. If he had possessed the calm resolution and settled judgment of his contemporary Archbishop of Canterbury, the result, not merely of the project for union, but of other movements then going on in the Gallican Church, might have been very different.

It chanced that about this time a Jansenist, Father Gerberon[2] published a work by one of the old school of Jansenists, Martin de Barcos, nephew of the well-known Abbé of St. Cyran, du Vergier de Hauranne. De Barcos had been dead seventeen years, and the publication of his work was an uncalled-for

[1] See Le Roy, pp. 8, 9.

[2] Dom Gerberon, first an Oratorian, then a Benedictine of St. Maur, was described by the Abbé Legendre (*Mémoires*, 232) as "the most eager and determined of Jansenists, as well as one of the most learned." His life was a stormy one. Louis XIV. tried to have him arrested at Corbie Abbey in 1682, but he escaped to Holland. In 1703 he was imprisoned at Amiens, at the instance of the Bishop of Malines, and afterwards at Vincennes. There he remained six years, not regaining his liberty till 1710. He died in 1711, at the age of eighty-three. See Le Roy, pp. 24-25.

attempt to re-open old controversies, and to disturb the existing settlement. But the dream of these "Calvinists saying mass," as the Jesuits called them, was to bring about a Reformation of the Gallican Church, in which individualist doctrines of grace might thrive side by side with the rites and ceremonies of Catholicism, both fostered by an unbroken hierarchy.[1]

It was inevitable that Gerberon's work, which appeared under the title of *Exposition de la Foi catholique touchant la Grâce et la Prédestination*, should draw upon itself hostile criticism. The copies of it found in Paris were ordered to be seized, and the Archbishop was applied to, to pronounce a formal condemnation of it. This he could not refuse to do; and accordingly, on August 20th, 1696, he issued an *Instruction pastorale*, in which it was duly censured. Then, when too late, he became aware of the trap that had been laid for him; of the horns of the dilemma on which he had impaled himself. If, as Bishop of Châlons, he had sanctioned the *Réflexions* of Quesnel, with what conscience could he now, as Archbishop of Paris, censure the *Exposition* of De Barcos? The enemies of De Noailles had not failed to spy their opportunity. Towards the end of 1698, there was printed surreptitiously at Brussels, for circulation in Paris early in the new year, a pamphlet of twenty-four pages, the title of which was out of all proportion to its size. It was, in full: *Problème ecclésiastique proposé à M. l'Abbé Boileau, de l'archevêché, à qui l'on doit croire de*

---

[1] Le Roy (p. 27 *n*) thinks that their aspirations may be seen realised, partly in the English Episcopal Church, and partly in the Old Catholic Church of Holland. This latter Church, known in Holland as the "oud-Roomsch," is, according to a recent writer, "in many ways an interesting body. Unlike most other sects, they remain just where they were on their separation from Rome. They have retained valid orders, the celibacy of the clergy, the Mass and other services in Latin. . . They profess to be not only Catholics, but Roman Catholics, and they acknowledge the Pope as the visible head of the Church, out of which there is no salvation." See the article on the "Jansenist Church of Holland" in Addis and Arnold's *Catholic Dictionary*, 1893. It will be remembered that it was from this Church that the first Bishop of the modern "Old Catholics," Dr. Joseph Hubert Reinkens, received his consecration. This was on August 11th, 1873, the consecrating Bishop being Dr. Heydekamp of Deventer.

Messire Louis-Antoine de Noailles, évêque de Châlons en 1695, *ou de Messire Louis-Antoine de Noailles, archevêque de Paris en* 1696. The object of the *brochure* is clear from the title. But behind the first "Problème" lies a second: who was the author? From which camp was the missile thrown; from that of the Jesuits? or from that of friends, from whom De Noailles might well have prayed to be saved, the more hot-headed Jansenists? Suspicion at first naturally pointed to the Jesuits. The Archbishop himself to the last believed the blow to have come from them. Saint-Simon, not very rationally, thought the author to be the Abbé J. J. Boileau himself, a friend of the Archbishop's. Jervis[1] thinks the writer was certainly Dom Thierri de Viaixne, whom D'Aguesseau calls a "Janseniste des plus outrés." But Le Roy has shown from the archives at Amersfoort that Dom Thierri, in a letter of October 20th, 1712, absolutely denies all knowledge of the *Problème*, and he comes to the conclusion, by arguments which we have not space to follow in detail, that the writer was a Jesuit, Père Doucin.[2]

The fate which immediately befel the *Problème* was to be publicly burnt in front of Notre Dame; and the Archbishop was cautioned by the King as to his relations with Quesnel. The impression naturally left on the popular mind was that De Noailles was an undoubted supporter of the Jansenists, and that any seeming coldness on his part towards them was the result of political necessity. As if to make compensation for any pain caused to De Noailles in this matter, Louis, before the end of the year, wrote a pressing letter to Innocent XII., recommending the Archbishop for advancement to the cardinalate. And when the hat came on July 22nd, 1700, the King, we are told, after hearing mass, took it from the hand of the Abbé de Barrière, and himself placed it on his favourite's head, with the words, "Je vous la donne de bon cœur, et je souhaite que vous en puissiez jouir longtemps."[3] In the course of this

---

[1] *Gallican Church*, ii. 93.
[2] *La France et Rome*, p. 59.
[3] *Mémoires du Marquis de Sourches*, vi. 275, quoted by Le Roy, p. 71 *n.*

same year, Innocent XII. died, and his successor, Clement XI., though naturally disposed to favour the Jesuits, had a kind feeling for the new Cardinal. The summer of 1700 must have been a season of hopeful anticipations for De Noailles.

But at the very time when he was absent at Rome for the conclave, an intrigue was being formed to entangle him in Paris. The plotters, on this occasion at least, are agreed to have been not Jesuits but Jansenists. But in this case, as in the one before mentioned, the implement of mischief was an anonymous pamphlet. Then it was the *Problème*, now a *Cas de Conscience*. The subject of the *Cas*, which was composed in 1701, but not published till the end of 1702, was briefly this:

A priest in the town of Normandy had been accustomed to hear the confessions of a brother ecclesiastic, and give him absolution, as being in a right state of heart and mind. But, suspicions having been raised as to the penitent's orthodoxy on points of Jansenism, he had questioned him closely under that head, and to his consternation had found that he was unsound on the five articles condemned by Innocent X. and Alexander VII. That is to say, he professed to condemn, *ex animo*, the propositions condemned; but, as to assigning the erroneous propositions to Jansenius as their author, he thought it sufficient to maintain a " respectful silence," not showing more obedience than this to the decision of the Popes.[1] When the confessor submitted the matter to the Doctors of the Sorbonne, asking their advice as to the way in which he should proceed, the general opinion was that the holding such tenets in the manner described did not present a bar to absolution; and the document, setting this forth, was signed by some forty of the Doctors.[2]

---

[1] Guetté, xi. 203 ; Le Roy, 94. Jervis adds some other tenets, as that " he did not believe the Pope to be infallible in matters of fact," and "upon several other controverted topics . . . he flatly contravened the favourite notions of the Jesuits."

[2] The form adopted was : " Les docteurs soussignés, qui ont vu l'exposé, sont d'avis que les sentiments de l'ecclésiastique dont il s'agit ne sont ni nouveaux, si singuliers, ni condamnés par l'Église, ni tels enfin que son confesseur doive exiger de lui qu'il les abandonne pour lui donner l'absolution. Délibéré en Sorbonne, ce 20 juillet, 1701."

STATE OF THE FRENCH CHURCH. 29

When this became known, by the publication of the *Cas de Conscience* at the end of 1702, as was said, or possibly a little later, fresh uneasiness was caused in the minds of French Churchmen. Jansenism had been thought dead, but here it was breaking out in fresh life in unexpected quarters. If forty Doctors of the Sorbonne could decide that the holding such opinions "did not matter," to what end were all the struggles and sufferings of the past half century? As the best way out of the difficulty, Bossuet suggested that the Doctors should be requested to recall their decision, and this suggestion was followed. Out of the forty, all but five were found to be accommodating. Of these five, the names of two will meet us in the correspondence, later on :—Ellies Du Pin and Nicolas Petitpied.[1]

The King, however, through the advice of his Jesuit counsellors, Père la Chaise and others, was becoming more and more convinced that nothing short of a fresh papal Bull would suffice to settle these disturbances once for all, and put a final stop to Jansenist heresies. Negotiations for this purpose went on through the year 1704. While foreign aid was thus being sought for the settlement of its home disputes, the French Church lost its brightest ornament, its staunchest defender, by the death of Bossuet. The venerable Bishop of Meaux breathed his last on April 12th, 1704, at the ripe age of

[1] Of Du Pin some account is given in the next chapter. Nicolas Petitpied was born in 1665. An uncle of the same name, who was himself a doctor in theology, brought him up in Gallican principles, and in due time sent him to the University of Paris. There he graduated with distinction, and rose, in 1701, to occupy a chair in the Sorbonne. It was from this post that he was now expelled, as a result of the part taken by him in the *Cas de Conscience*. From 1705 to 1718 he shared the exile of Quesnel. After being recalled to his native country at the last-mentioned date, he was banished a second time, in 1728, and finally died, though not in exile, in 1747. The Bishop of Senez, writing in 1718, bore witness to the attractive qualities of the "pieux pèlerin":—"Dieu vous a donné le talent de dorer ce que vous touchez, et de porter le jour parmi les ténèbres." In the archives at Amersfoort there is said to exist a voluminous correspondence of Petitpied, ranging over a number of years from 1703 onwards.—See Le Roy, pp. 115-116.

seventy-seven years. With his death, as his biographer truly observes, begins a new epoch in the history of the French Church.[1] His learning, his blameless life, his force of character, joined to his paramount influence with the King, had enforced the respect of both the great parties in that Church, and compelled them, to some extent, to an armistice. When this powerful control was removed, the suppressed jealousies broke out into open war.

The appeal to Rome, which Bossuet, had he lived, might have been able to avert, came to an issue in the following year, by the publication, July 17th, 1705, of the Bull *Vineam Domini Sabaoth*. It may seem strange that at such a period of foreign wars the mind of the French King should have been so absorbed in ecclesiastical affairs; that in the very year of Blenheim he should have been busy in gaining the opinions of his law officers on the draft of this Bull. Some writers have loved to trace in it the work of an avenging nemesis; an infatuation which followed on the harsh treatment of the Protestant communities; a weakness caused by the draining away of the best blood of the country at the Revocation of the Edict of Nantes.[2]

Be this as it may, the King must have thought his efforts for the consolidation of the Church crowned with success, when, on the 3rd of August, at the meeting of the Assembly of the Clergy in Paris, he was able to lay before them the Bull *Vineam Domini*. It had cost much to obtain it. The Pope had been compelled to use such caution in drawing it up, for fear of offending Gallican sensibilities, that it seemed at one time as if the scheme would have to be abandoned altogether.

[1] "Un nouveau siècle s'ouvroit ; et déjà se répandoit cet esprit inquiet et novateur, dont le nom de Bossuet avoit pu seul jusqu'alors contenir l'audace et les témérités. Deux partis divisoient alors l'Église de France. Tous les deux, en affectant de respecter l' autorité de Bossuet, étaient impatiens de se soustraire à l'espèce de dictature que l'opinion publique lui avoit déférée. Il avoit toujours su réprimer leurs écarts, et les contenir dans les bornes qu'ils n'auroient jamais dû franchir pour leur propre intérêt." Bausset : *Histoire de Bossuet*, 1819, tom. iv., p. 426.

[2] Comp. *La Reforme en Saintonge*, par E. Moutarde, 1892, pp. 16, *sqq*.

Louis, on his side, had thought it so needful to persist in the demand, as to assure the Pope, that, if the document were not ready by the next meeting of the Clergy, the Assembly might take the law into its own hands, and itself frame the decision which had in vain been waited for from Rome.[1] Great, then, must have been the vexation, both of King and Pope, when the Assembly, with the Archbishop of Paris at its head, instead of humbly and gratefully accepting the Bull as it was, spent a week or ten days in debating upon it, and ended by laying down certain articles, conditional to their acceptance.[2] After the Bull had been accepted, subject to these provisos, the Assembly concluded its session with a letter to the Pope, in which ceremonious language only half concealed the chafing under dictation from without.

To punish De Noailles, who was looked upon both at the French Court[3] and in Rome as the head and front of the resistance, he was required by the King's express order to tender the Bull, thus received by the clergy, to the sisterhood of Port Royal for their acceptance. It was a cruel and arbitrary measure. The sisters of that community had done nothing to deserve any severity, and if punishment must be inflicted on them, it was doubly hard that the hand of De Noailles should be chosen to inflict it.

The Convent of Port Royal des Champs, near Chevreuse, had been an example of an institution sinking to the lowest

[1] Le Roy, 176.
[2] These were: "1° Que les évêques ont droit, par institution divine, de juger des matières de doctrine; 2° Que les constitutions des papes obligent toute l'église, lorsqu'elles ont été acceptées par le corps des pasteurs; 3° Que cette acceptation de la part des évêques se fait toujours par voie de jugement."
[3] Madame de Maintenon, from being a warm friend of the Archbishop's, had by this time become his active enemy. He was connected with her by the marriage of his nephew, the Comte d'Ayen, with her niece, Françoise d'Aubigny. The Life of Mme. de Maintenon was written by her grand-nephew, the Duc de Noailles, and an interesting review of the work by J. J. Ampère appeared in the *Revue des deux Mondes*, Nov. 15th, 1848, and was afterwards included in Ampère's collected works. See his *Mélanges*, 1867, tom. ii., pp. 491-523.

depths, but mercifully raised again, and restored to fresh beauty and fresh usefulness. At the close of the sixteenth century it was "like the majority of the religious houses in France, in a state of scandalous degeneracy. Its professed rule was ignored; the nuns had ceased to observe even the law of seclusion; the prescribed routine of daily devotion and ascetic exercises was exchanged for habits of frivolous amusement and luxurious indulgence."[1] In 1599, Marie Angélique Arnauld, a child of eight, was made coadjutrix to the Abbess. In 1602, when just eleven, she was herself consecrated Abbess. Yet this event, which must have seemed but an accumulation of abuses, was destined to be, humanly speaking, the salvation of the community. Six years later, Angélique experienced a profound change in her religious feelings. She was convinced that her vocation was to purify and reform the body over which she had been called to preside. In brief, she restored the Benedictine rule in all its integrity in the Abbey of Des Champs, and lived to see the example followed through many a religious house in the north of France. In 1627 the convent was withdrawn from the jurisdiction of the Abbot of Citeaux, and placed under that of the Archbishop of Paris,—a step destined, as we shall see, to produce the most serious mischief. So far the sisters of Port Royal had not been distinguished by any peculiar religious opinions; but circumstances, which it would be too long here to relate, brought Angélique into connexion with Du Verger de Hauranne, the famous Abbot of St. Cyran. St. Cyran obtained from Jansenius a formal approbation of a work drawn up for use at Port Royal, and in 1636 was himself made director of the institution. Thus it was that a suspicion of Jansenism came to hang over the convent. But in 1668, when a compromise between contending parties had been arrived at in what was known as the "Peace of Clement," Port Royal had escaped molestation, being allowed to declare its adhesion to orthodoxy in a qualified sense.

Unhappily for the sisterhood, the King coveted their endow-

[1] Jervis, i. 339.

STATE OF THE FRENCH CHURCH.

ments, and his mind had been prejudiced against them by the foes of Jansenism. De Noailles, therefore, was to take the preliminary step of requiring their acceptance of the provisions of the Bull *Vineam Domini;* a humiliation to himself, a snare to them. They replied by offering to subscribe it, with the reservation that had been allowed them in the time of Clement IX. This was refused. Nor would they have been in better case, had they subscribed unconditionally. It was the old story of the wolf and the lamb. In 1706 the abbess was prohibited by royal mandate from receiving novices for the future.[1] Step by step, resistance was crushed. In March, 1708, Clement XI. himself joined in the work of destruction by a Bull, suppressing the Abbey of Port Royal des Champs, and annexing its property to the sister institution in Paris. This was but making the two morsels into one, to be swallowed together. On the representations of Le Tellier, successor to Père la Chaise in the office of King's confessor, Louis was persuaded that no wholesome rule could be maintained in the joint community, and that the nuns had better be dispersed through other convents, and the "nest of heresy" scattered to the winds. The King's mandate was issued accordingly; and, as if the task would be a perilous one, a force of 300 armed men supported the Marquis d'Argenson, lieutenant of police, in the execution of it. The nuns were hastily conveyed away to other religious houses, there to be kept in a state of penance. The conventual buildings, in 1710, were levelled to the ground, and the very graveyard of the sisterhood rifled, the remains of those interred there being hurriedly and indecently removed. The churches of neighbouring parishes contain memorials of the spoliation. The Marquis de Pomponne was able to save the remains of some of his relatives, the glory of Port Royal, the Arnaulds, and re-inter them in the Church of Palaiseau. There may still be seen, over their changed resting-place, the pathetic epitaph: *Tandem requiescant.*[2]

No wonder that Cardinal de Noailles, though he had been

[1] Jervis, ii. 188. [2] Le Roy, p. 288; Jervis, ii. 191; Guettée, xi 248.

more sinned against than sinning, felt weighed down by the consciousness of the part he had taken in this heinous work. "Few scenes in history" writes Jervis, "are more affecting than that drawn by the annalists of Port Royal of the Cardinal's pilgrimage to the ruins of the desecrated sanctuary. Scourged by ceaseless remorse, he resolved to seek relief by an act of solemn penance performed on the spot. He proceeded thither, attended only by his secretary Thomassin, a faithful monitor, who had earnestly laboured to dissuade him from the policy which now weighed so intolerably on his conscience. On reaching the site of the abbey, he became completely unnerved by emotion; his lamentations were piteous; he was convulsed by tears and sobs. Wringing his hands in an agony of grief, he cast himself upon the ground, and cried aloud to heaven for mercy. 'O,' said he, 'all these dismantled stones will rise up against me at the day of judgment! O how shall I ever endure this vast, this heavy load!' It was with difficulty that the secretary succeeded in replacing him in his carriage, and bringing him back to Paris. Nor does it appear that the poignancy of his compunction was much assuaged by the lapse of time. He was heart-broken; sinking at times into a settled gloom not far removed from despair."[1]

The whole episode is a painful one; but it is instructive for our present purpose, as showing to what depths of bitterness religious partizanship could proceed, and as helping to explain the strong aversion with which the Jesuits before many years came to be regarded in France. A sense of the cruel way in which he had been entrapped was doubtless fresh in the mind of De Noailles, when, in the next year, 1711, he refused to renew the certificates for preaching and hearing confessions held by Jesuits in his diocese,—at least, by those who had made themselves specially obnoxious.[2]

---

[1] *Gallican Church*, ii., p. 193, quoting Pontain and the Abbé Grégoire. Soanen, Bishop of Senez, used to say that in the troubles which soon gathered thickly about De Noailles, he saw the stones of Port Royal hanging over his head.

[2] Le Roy, p. 365.

But we must hasten to the event which, more than any other, prepared the way for the temporary contact of the French and English churches. This was the publication of the Bull *Unigenitus*.

According to Father Lafiteau, whose evidence will not be suspected of any partiality for Jansenism, the renewal of dissensions on that subject was due to the action of two Bishops, De Lescure of Luçon, and Champflour of La Rochelle, who published conjointly, in July, 1710, an *Ordonnance et Instruction Pastorale*, containing fresh denunciations of the *Réflexions Morales* of Quesnel.[1] According to some, the real instigator of the movement was a Capucin monk, Timothée de la Flèche by name, known afterwards as the "courrier de la Bulle." The *Instruction* was printed at La Rochelle, and, as soon as it was ready, copies were dispersed about the kingdom, Paris, of course, receiving its full share. The bookseller who acted as publisher's agent in the capital, posted up notices of the publication in the usual places, and also on the gates of the Archbishop's palace. Lafiteau labours to show that there was nothing irregular in this last proceeding, but admits that it would have been in better taste, under the circumstances, not to placard the Archbishop's gates. That the proceeding was improper, if not wantonly insulting, seems clear from what followed. De Noailles fired up at the affront, and took the unfortunate course of insisting on the expulsion from the Seminary of St. Sulpice of two young students there, whose only fault was that each was a nephew of one of the two Bishops. So unjust and impolitic a step would have gone far to turn the tide of public favour away from the Archbishop, but for his two opponents putting themselves almost equally in the wrong by an intemperate and unwarrantable accusation of him in a letter to the King.

The acrimony with which the dispute was carried on, helped to convince Louis that no permanent settlement of it

---

[1] "Il est vraisemblable qu'il donna lieu à la querelle qui divise aujourd'hui l'Épiscopat." *Hist. de la Constitution*, i., p. 99.

could be obtained without having recourse to the Holy See. He was himself now old and infirm, more capable of holding tenaciously to a purpose than of originating anything fresh. And the question has hence been raised, from what quarter the suggestions came which had now taken possession of the royal mind. Lafiteau strives to show that the first move was made by De Noailles, or, at least, that it was made with his consent.[1] But St. Simon is probably right in pointing to Le Tellier and his party as the real originators:—" What he desired was, to make it an affair of so much embroilment and dissension, that it should be of necessity carried to Rome, contrary to all the laws and usages of the Church, which provide that such questions shall be decided judicially on the spot where they originate, saving the right of appeal to the Pope."[2]

Whatever motives may have prompted the King's action, he went on with settled determination in the course he had chosen; and it is interesting for our purpose to notice the way in which the "Gallican liberties" came to be more and more infringed. In November, 1711, the further sale and circulation of Quesnel's book was prohibited by an *arrêt* of the Council of State. D'Aguesseau, the Avocat-Général, and Pontchartrain, the Chancellor, both ventured to argue against the measure as unconstitutional; seeing that the papal Brief, previously condemning the alleged errors of the *Réflexions* had been held to violate the liberties of the Gallican Church. The present *arrêt* would be considered to sanction that Brief. But this remonstrance had no effect, and in December of that year, the King, through his chargé d'affaires at Rome, Cardinal Tremoille, made formal application for a Bull, "distinctly

---

[1] "Ce fut donc du consentement, ou même par le conseil de M. le Cardinal de Noailles, que le Livre du P. Quênel fut porté au Tribunal du St. Siège." *Histoire*, i., p. 116.

[2] *Mémoires*, tom. vi., p. 412, quoted by Jervis, ii. 207. It should be added that St. Simon goes on to explain the last clause by saying that the "judicial form" in which the Pope on appeal can correct or affirm a judgment appealed against, is by a Council, at which the accused person can appear. Quesnel constantly asked for this.

specifying and condemning the errors contained in the *Nouveau Testament* of Quesnel, which the decree of 1708 had only censured in general terms." [1]

It is alleged by St. Simon, on the authority of M. Amelot, a councillor of state despatched by the French Government to Rome, that it was from the first not the wish of Clement XI. to put forth any constitution on the subject. It is said that he even went so far as to declare that the specification of so many errors was forced upon him in order to satisfy Cardinal Fabroni, and sustain the credit of Le Tellier.[2] But whether this was so or not, the task was undertaken in compliance with the French King's request, and Quesnel's work was exposed to a searching investigation. After it had been sifted at seventeen conferences of theologians, and at twenty-four congregations, at which the Pope himself and nine Cardinals were present, the unhappy subject of the inquest was found guilty of containing no fewer than a hundred and one heretical or erroneous propositions.[3] Accordingly, on September 8th, 1713, with all due formalities,[4] the Bull beginning with the words *Unigenitus Dei Filius* was launched in condemnation of them.

It would be beside our purpose to discuss the doctrines here condemned, or the soundness of the theology with which they are declared to be inconsistent. It may suffice to say that the most serious error pronounced against appears to be the Jansenist tenet of the irresistible nature of Divine grace. What we have to observe is the way in which the Bull was refused acceptance by defenders of the rights of the French Church.

When the Bull was received in France, the King consulted with his advisers as to the proper mode of bringing it before

---

[1] Jervis, ii. 209. [2] *Ib.*, ii. 226.
[3] The text of the Bull itself, with a schedule of the propositions condemned, has been often reprinted, and need not be given here. It will be found prefixed to the first volume of Lafiteau's *Histoire*, and also at the end of Le Roy's *France et Rome*.
[4] Lafiteau, i. 144.

the clergy for their acceptance. The constitutional way, which De Noailles and others recommended, was by provincial synods. But Louis seems to have thought it would be more expeditious to summon to an Assembly all such prelates as were in or near Paris at the time.[1] Accordingly, on October 4th, this method was agreed to by the Council, and the notices sent out. The meeting was called for the 16th; Cardinal de Noailles was to be the president. At the first sitting, twenty-nine bishops or archbishops were present. Twenty-three more subsequently joined them, making, as Le Roy computes, rather more than a third, but less than half, of the French episcopate.[2]

Though it had been fondly hoped that the Assembly would be unanimous, it soon became evident that there were serious differences of opinion in it on the subject of the reception of the Bull. The main body would have accepted it without question, out of respect for the Holy See, and in deference to the King's wishes. But right and left of this were two wings, one of which would have submitted to the Pope's decision in the matter, as to an infallible authority, while the other, headed by the president, did not feel conscientiously able to accept the Bull, unless certain qualifications or explanations of it were first made. They would have repeated, in short, what had already been done in case of the Bull *Vineam Domini*. A committee, to which the matter was referred, reported, on January 13th, 1714, that the Bull should be accepted, with the addition of an "Instruction pastorale," to be drawn up and approved in common, in which the explanations desired should be given. Naturally, De Noailles and those who thought with him declined to subscribe to this

---

[1] Le Roy, p. 479. The suggestion is there ascribed to Le Tellier.

[2] *Ib.*, p. 485. Fénelon, writing to his nephew the Marquis de Fénelon, September 11th, 1713, speculates with eager interest on the reception the bull would have. "Il est fort à désirer," he says, "qu'on voie une acceptation unanime de tous : mais enfin, quand même il arriverait qu'une douzaine d'évêques refuseraient d'accepter sans quelque clause restrictive, le torrent prévaudrait."—*Œuvres*, 1857, iii., p. 712.

until the "Instruction" was forthcoming; and when it was produced, on February 1st, the same party refused their assent to it, and the whole matter was brought to a standstill.

The subject of the Bull was now becoming a topic of excited discussion in Paris, and many a passing epigram was shot at

"Ce brief qui fait tant de fracas."

On February 5th the protesting bishops addressed a long letter to the King, explaining the reasons of the course they had adopted. It suited his purpose best, however, to take but very slight notice of this, and to affect that the Assembly had earned his thanks and compliments for their unanimous compliance with his wishes. By an exercise of pressure reminding us of an earlier Tudor sovereign, Louis secured the registration of the Bull in Parliament, and then proceeded to take the Sorbonne in like manner by storm.

Here, however, he met with an unexpected resistance. Cardinal de Noailles was "Provisor" of the Sorbonne as well as Archbishop of Paris; and a *mandement* from him to the doctors caused them to hesitate seriously before complying with the King's desire. The usual monthly meeting of the Faculty came on the 1st of March; and thereupon, at half-past eight in the morning, two hundred Doctors of Divinity assembled. The full number should have been over two hundred and fifty, but apprehension of future troubles might probably keep many away.[1] Proceedings began by the reading of the *lettre de cachet*, and a fervid address from the Syndic Le Rouge, adjuring the members to reject the pestilent stock (*la damnable souche*) of heresy. But the assembly was by no means enthusiastic in the cause. The votes were divided, and at adjourned meetings on the 3rd and 5th no greater unanimity prevailed. The Molinist faction resorted to threats, interruptions, almost to actual violence. Cries of "Læsa Majestas," "Ejiciatur," "Manifesta rebellio in regem" resounded through the hall.[2]

[1] Le Roy, p. 575, quoting *Rélation des Délibérations*, p. 20.
[2] Petitpied of Vaubreuil, writing on March 3rd to his brother Nicolas (of whom see above, p. 29), cannot find words to describe the scene in the

The Jesuit Gaillande was found eavesdropping in the building, and was summarily expelled. To quell opposition to the King's mandate, the secretary was ordered to register the votes under two headings, those of "acceptants" and "adversaries to the King." Any remonstrance was met with a chorus of "Mentiris." But it was not till after a sixth meeting, on April 17th, 1714, that the Sorbonne finally gave in. On May 1st the Bull was accepted by the Faculty, with only fourteen dissentients; and from that day till the death of Louis XIV. "silence weighed heavy on the Sorbonne."[1]

Even this success had not been obtained without the banishment of a number of the members; a step which did not tend to make the Bull more popular in France. Outside the bounds of the kingdom the interest taken in it was very languid. Of 466 archbishops and bishops in other Catholic countries, Le Roy calculates that only twenty two or twenty-three helped to promulgate the constitution. It was ignored by the Orthodox Greek Church. "Among Protestants and among Eastern Christians alike, the appearance of the Bull called forth renewed hostility to Rome, from which had come so unexpected a justification of the schism of Photius, and the Reformation of Luther."[2] The learned Church historian, Basnage, when asked his opinion of the measure, replied: "It will be a matter of triumph for us, and we shall find in it proofs of several arguments hitherto employed by us to justify our separation, and to establish the defection of the Church of Rome."

In face of the strong opposition to the Bull—for, though the Bishops, Parliament, and the Sorbonne had been coerced or won over, it was still most unpopular with parish priests, many religious orders, and the laity at large—the Jesuit party were perplexed what course to take. Their great supporter, Fénelon, was using the brief remainder, as it proved, of his life, to

Sorbonne on that day. "Je sors de l'enfer," he says: "la salle de Sorbonne était aujourd'hui l'enfer." Le Roy, p. 577, from the archives at Amersfoort.

[1] Le Roy, p. 586. [2] *Ib.*, p. 595.

advocate the calling of a National or a General Council.[1] His friends made no secret of their conviction that, in case such a Council could be held, none else would be so fit as he to take his seat at it as Papal legate. But for such an anticipation, they would hardly have welcomed a scheme, which, as one says,[2] might have proved "an emancipation big with results; one that might have inspired the ecclesiastical organization of France with fresh life, fresh youth, and been a step on the road towards the establishment of national churches."

The scheme of a National Council of the Gallican Church was taken up by the King. Louis thought he had found a most promising envoy to the Papal Court, to obtain the sanction of Clement XI., in M. Amelot, "one of the best heads in France," as he is called by Mathieu Marais, a friend of the Jesuits, but a man of honour, one who had been a successful chargé d'affaires at Venice, Madrid, Lisbon, and elsewhere. But two causes proved fatal to the mission. Amelot set off on December 12th, 1714, and arrived in Rome on January 9th in the new year. But two days before that, the Archbishop of Cambrai had breathed his last. This materially lessened the interest of the Jesuits in the project of a Council, as they felt that there was no one to take Fénelon's place.

At Rome, moreover, Amelot met with nothing but disappointment. Le Père Timothée, of whom mention has been made before,[3] had, or pretended to have, the Pope's ear. The French envoy, Cardinal de Tremoille, was jealous of this person, and both alike were distrustful of Amelot. By a master-stroke of policy, Amelot succeeded in getting the

---

[1] The title of one tract written by him was: *Mémoire sur la nécessité et les moyens de ramener le cardinal de Noailles et les autres prélats réfractaires à l'avis de l'assemblée du clergé;* of another: *Sur les motifs qui doivent engager le Saint-Siège à envoyer la constitution Unigenitus à toutes les églises catholiques.*

[2] Le Roy, p. 613.

[3] *Supra*, p. 35.

Capucin monk made Bishop of Berytus, and Coadjutor of the Bishop of Babylon, which at any rate got him away from Rome. But there still remained to be dealt with the impracticable temper of the Pope. Between him and Cardinal Fabroni, even the experienced Amelot found himself baffled, and the year 1715 was wearing away in fruitless negotiations. The lowest point of De Noailles's fortune seemed to be reached in April, 1715, when "a brief was addressed to him, through the Nuncio, commanding him to notify his acceptance of the Constitution, 'pure et simple,' within fifteen days, under pain of being degraded from the Roman purple, and proceeded against according to the canons."[1] But it is doubted whether this letter was ever, in fact, delivered by the Nuncio.

Impatient of further delay, Louis XIV. had determined, like another Henry VIII., to take the law into his own hands, and summon a National Council of the French Church himself, when death intervened. On July 24th, 1715, the Chancellor Voysin officially notified the King's intention. On August 11th came the news from Marly that the King was "not so well." On the morning of September 1st, as all know, the long reign of Louis Quatorze was ended by his death.

With the faults or the virtues of the Grand Monarque we are not now concerned. The Jesuits had good cause to lament his death, for of late years, at any rate, his counsels had been almost exclusively guided by them. To content them, and to enforce the acceptance of the *Unigenitus*, he had banished, or sent to the Bastille, Bishops and Doctors of the Sorbonne. With the Regency, under the Duc d'Orléans, came a sudden change. De Tellier and his party found themselves looked coldly on at Court. The smiles of royal favour shone for a time again on De Noailles.

---

[1] Jervis, ii. 227. The expressive French terms were, that he should be *dénaturalisé* in France, and *décardinalisé* at Rome. Le Roy, p. 632. There are among the Additional MSS. in the British Museum (No. 20,310, etc.), many volumes of letters to and from the Papal Nuncio at the French Court about this time, Cardinal Antonio Filippo Gualterio, the one referred to in the text.

It was at this juncture, when the wind had shifted, but the sky was still overcast, that the course of affairs in the French Church was brought for a short time into contact with that of our own.

CHAPTER III.
Correspondence between Archbishop Wake and others.

WHILE such was the state of things in France, a correspondence began between Wake, Archbishop of Canterbury, and friends in that country, which seemed likely at one time to lead to important results. We might almost dignify the correspondence, in its later stages, with the title of negotiations, but for the distinct understanding, more than once expressed by the English representative, that what he wrote must not be taken to bear any official character. As the highest ecclesiastic, however, in the Church of England, it was impossible for the words of Archbishop Wake to be regarded as merely private or informal; and the weight attaching to them from his official position was increased by the knowledge of his previous career.

William Wake, a native of Blandford in Dorsetshire, had entered Christ Church, Oxford, in 1672, being then only in his sixteenth year. After graduating at the usual time, and choosing divinity as his profession, he was ordained, and in 1682 accompanied Viscount Preston, another old Christ Church man, to Paris, in the capacity of chaplain. Lord Preston had been appointed English envoy at the Court of France. Wake would thus enter the French capital in the very year when a synod of the clergy there assembled performed, to use Dr. Dorner's words,[1] "the most celebrated act of Gallicanism," in putting forth the *Declaratio Cleri Gallicani*. Besides having his attention thus turned to the French Church, at an exciting moment of her history, Wake became favourably known as a scholar to many of the French savants,

[1] Article in the *Contemporary Review*, vol. xvii., p. 601.

and was applied to by Bishop Fell to collate some MSS. of the Greek Testament in Paris for the use of Mill's intended edition. He had even ventured to break a lance with no less redoubtable an opponent than Bossuet, Bishop of Meaux. In 1671, appeared Bossuet's *Exposition de la Foi Catholique*, a work esteemed of so much importance, as to be afterwards incorporated in the great *Recueil des Actes . . . du Clergé de France*. But when examined, on its first publication, by the Doctors of the Sorbonne, so many points in it were marked for censure, that the whole impression was withdrawn, as far as practicable, and a fresh one issued before the end of the same year. In this no notice of the original edition was taken. Wake, into whose hands a copy of that first impression had fallen, was thus able to retort upon the author of the *Histoire des Variations des Églises Protestantes.* This he did in the preface to his *Exposition of the Doctrine of the Church of England*, which appeared in 1686. He recurred to the same subject afterwards, in a sermon preached before William and Mary at Hampton Court, in May, 1689, when he took occasion to point out the variations of doctrine among Roman Catholics themselves. "How vain, then," he added, "must that argument be, which a late Author of the Church of Rome has with so much pomp revived against us."[1]

Before this, in 1688, soon after his return to England with Viscount Preston, Wake had been chosen Preacher of Gray's Inn. It was in keeping with the encroaching spirit shown by James II., in this last year of his reign, that he sent a message, we are told,[2] to the Benchers of Gray's Inn, desiring them not to proceed to an election till they heard from him. They were fortunate in being able to answer, "that they had already chosen Dr. Wake."

It is worthy of notice that Dr. William Claget, whom Wake succeeded in the Preachership of this Inn, was himself known

[1] *Sermon on Rom.* xv. 5-7, Lond. 1689, p. 9.
[2] See the art. WAKE in the *Biographia Britannica*. The authority there given for this statement, is "Mr. Beauvoir of Canterbury," a son of the Archbishop's correspondent in France.

as a writer in the controversy with the Church of Rome. In 1687 he had published an account of the books written on both sides, under the title of *The Present State of the Controversie between the Church of England and the Church of Rome;* and this, which was itself a continuation of a work begun by Tenison, was taken up and enlarged by Wake in 1688, under the heading, *A Continuation of the Present State of the Controversy.* That one who was to succeed Tenison in the highest office of the English Church should succeed him in this earlier task, seems worthy of remark.

In 1693 Wake published his translation of the *Epistles of the Apostolical Fathers*,[1] chiefly with the view of exhibiting the state of Church government in primitive times. In the same year he was made Rector of St. James's, Westminster, and began now to take a prominent part in the disputes about Convocation. In support of the control exercised by the sovereign, in this country, over the meetings of Convocation, he published, in 1697, *The Authority of Christian Princes over their Ecclesiastical Synods;* and, in 1703, in opposition to Atterbury, his great work, the *State of the Church and Clergy of England.* In this year he was made Bishop of Lincoln, and in January, 1716, on the death of Tenison, was translated to the see of Canterbury.

For an apparent inconsistency of conduct in his discharge of these two high offices, Wake has been often censured.[2] As Bishop of Lincoln, he had "distinguished himself by a long and learned speech in favour of a comprehension with dissenters." But in 1718 he voted and spoke in the House of Lords against the repeal of the Schism and Conformity Bill, and in the following year, on the same principle, he opposed the repeal of the Corporation and Test Acts. To ascribe this change to the difference in his own rank or position is emi-

---

[1] *The Genuine Epistles of St. Barnabas, St. Ignatius, St. Clement, St. Polycarp, the Shepherd of Hermas,* etc. *Translated and published in English.* London, 1693, 8vo.

[2] "The inconsistency," say the authors of *The English Church in the Eighteenth Century*, "is a blemish in his character."

nently unfair.[1] At no time of his life was his pen busier in fraternal correspondence with the representatives of foreign Protestant communities.[2] It is not likely that he would have voted against the relaxation of legal restrictions on the nonconformists of his own country, if he had not discerned some dangers in the spirit in which that relaxation was now sought.

Whatever we may think of the judgment shown by Archbishop Wake in this matter, it will be clear, from what has been said, that he was specially qualified, by study and inclination, to be the spokesman of the English Church in the negotiations, if such they may be called, that were about to be opened with divines of the Church of France. The circumstances which led to this interchange of opinions must now be briefly related.

The chaplain to Lord Stair, English ambassador at the French Court during the years with which we are concerned, was the Rev. William Beauvoir, M.A., of Christ's College, Cambridge.[3] As occupying the same position that Wake had occupied thirty years before, it was natural that he should be known to the Archbishop, with whom we find him in correspondence in 1717. He enjoyed, moreover, the friendship of Du Pin,[4] De Girardin,[5] and other distinguished members of

---

[1] See Perry, *History of the Church of England*, iii. 309. It is noticeable that a like inconsistency was laid to the charge of Cardinal de Noailles, with regard to his opinion of Quesnel's work, when Bishop of Châlons in 1695, and when Archbishop of Paris in 1696. This gave rise to a *jeu d'esprit*, on the question "à qui l'on doit croire."—See Jervis, ii., p. 92.

[2] Compare his letter to Le Clerc, April 8th, 1718: "Unionem inter omnes Reformatos procurare quovis pacto vellem. . . . Sed abripuit me longius quam par esset, hæc semper mihi dulcis de pace ac unione Ecclesiarum Reformatarum cogitatio." *Wake Corresp.*, vol. cclviii., No. 9. To the same effect a letter to Turretin, a little earlier, *ib.*, No. 6.

[3] Rector of Bocking, in Essex, 1719; died 1723.

[4] Louis Ellies Du Pin is said to have been born June 17th, 1657, of a noble family in Normandy. He took his Bachelor's degree in 1684, and his Doctor's in 1686. He is best known by his great work, the *Nouvelle Bibliothèque des Auteurs ecclésiastiques*, of which thirty-five volumes appeared between 1698 and 1711. Some additional volumes are mentioned in the course of this correspondence. He died June 6th, 1719.

[5] This Doctor of the Sorbonne is said to have originally borne the

the Gallican Church. On the 8th of April, 1717, Du Pin wrote to Beauvoir a letter, in which, after commending to him a M. du Bussy, he adds, as a piece of information that will interest his correspondent, the fact of four bishops having appealed against the Bull *Unigenitus*, and of their appeal being concurred in by the Theological Faculty of Paris.[1]

"Je ne scais," he writes, "si vous scaués que quatre Eueques, scauoir M^{grs} de Mirepaux [Mirepoix], de Senez, de Montpelier et de Boulogne, ont appellé de la Constitution *Unigenitus;* qu'ils sont venus le 5e mars dernier apporter leur acte d'appel à lassemblée de notre facultée; quelle la approuve et y adhere. . . . Voila des nouuelles que ne vous seront pas indifferentes."[2]

The earliest letter of Beauvoir to the Archbishop, that appears to have been preserved, is one dated December 11th (O. S.), 1717. It is in answer to one from Wake, dated Lambeth, November 28th (O. S.), of the same year, in which the subjects referred to are simply literary. Beauvoir, after acknowledging what the Archbishop had written under this head, adds that Du Pin and some other doctors of the Sorbonne, with whom he had been dining,

"talked as if the whole kingdom was to appeal to the future general council, etc. They wished for an union with the Church of England, as the most effectual means to unite all the western churches. Dr. Du Pin desired me to give his duty to your Grace, upon my telling him that I would send you an *arrêt* of the Parliament of Paris relating to him, and a small tract of his."[3]

name of Patrick Piers only, and to have added the surname of De Girardin "to denote his extraction from a family of that name in Ireland." —See the Oxford edition of Courayer's *Dissertation*, 1844, p. xiv *n.*

[1] One effect of the favour shown to De Noailles by the Regent was to encourage the appellant bishops and their party in the opposition to the Bull. "The spirit of resistance," says Jervis (ii. 234), "showed itself in a formidable shape in March, 1717, when four bishops, De la Broue of Mirepoix, Soanen of Senez, Colbert of Montpellier, and Delangle of Boulogne, executed a solemn act of appeal to a future General Council against the Bull Unigenitus."

[2] *Beauvoir Corresp.*, No. 4. The spelling of the French has not been modernized.

[3] Dec. 11th (O. S.), 1717. Quoted by Maclaine, p. 174.

Wake appears to have replied to this, in a letter not preserved, making courteous reference to Du Pin.[1] In acknowledging this courtesy, Du Pin wrote, on February 11th, 1718, expressing an ardent desire for union between Churches so little separated as the Anglican and Gallican:

"Unum addam cum bona venia tua, me vehementer optare, ut unionis inter Ecclesias anglicanam et gallicanam ineundæ via aliqua inveniri posset. Non ita sumus ab invicem in plerisque dissiti, ut non possimus mutuo reconciliari. Atque utinam Christiani omnes essent unum ovile."[2]

As this letter appears to have been forwarded to the Archbishop by Mr. Beauvoir, inclosed in one of his own, it was to the latter that Wake addressed his reply. The first overtures, as we see, had come from the French side. Wake, with every disposition to welcome them, felt that caution was necessary. His letter shall be given entire:[3]

"*Feb.* 14 (*S. V.*) 1717 [*in New Style*, 1718].
"REVEREND SIR,

"When I received the favour of yours, with that of M\[r\] Du Pin enclosed, I was confined to my Chamber with a painfull distemper, which, bringing a feavour along with it, has very much broke my spirits, and made me altogether unfit hitherto for businesse. But that I may not seem to neglect such a friendly invitation as that D\[r\] made me to a future Correspondence, I have by the enclosed answered it, rather as I was able under my present circumstances, than as I would otherwise have wish'd to do. The D\[r\] mentions one Volume already publish'd of Protestant writers criticised by him, to the year 1600, and of another ready to come out.[4] I must get them as soon as he has finish'd what he designs in that Argument.

---

[1] "En répondant à cette dernière lettre, Mgr Wake fait une mention honorable de M. Du Pin, qu'il regarde comme un auteur de mérite, et il exprime le désir de lui rendre service."—*D'un Projet d'union*, p. 1.
[2] Maclaine, p. 146.
[3] *Beauvoir Corresp.*, No. 3.
[4] This refers to the volumes of the *Bibliothèque des Auteurs separez de la Communion de l'Église Romaine*, of which tom. i., in two volumes, appeared in 1718, and tom. ii., also in two volumes, in 1719. See the note above, p. 47.

Pray make my compliments and excuses to the D^r, and assure him that whatever else he may exceed me in, he shall not do it in a true respect for his person, nor in a hearty zeal for the peace and unity of the Church of Christ.

"The Church of England, as a national Church, has all that power within herselfe over her own members, which is necessary to enable her to settle her doctrines, government, and discipline, according to the will of Christ and the edification of her members. We have no concern for other Christian Churches more than that of charity, and to keep up the unity of the Catholic Church in the Communion of Saints. The Church of France, if it would once in good earnest throw off the Pope's pretensions, has the same right and independence. She may establish a different worship, discipline, &c., and in some points continue to differ from us in doctrine too, and yet maintain a true communion with us, so long as there is nothing either in her worship or ours to hinder the members of each Church to communicate with the other, as they have opportunity.

"I make no doubt but that a plan might be framed to bring the Gallican Church to such a state, that we might each hold a true Catholic Unity and communion with one another, and yet each continue in many things to differ, as we see the Protestant Churches do; nay, as both among them and us many learned men do differ in several very considerable points from each other. To frame a common confession of faith, or liturgie, or discipline, for both Churches, is a project never to be accomplish'd. But to settle each so that the other shall declare it to be a sound part of the Catholic Church, and communicate with one another as such;—this may easily be done without much difficulty by them abroad, and I make no doubt but the best and wisest of our Church would be ready to give all due encouragement to it.

"You cannot err in encouraging them to draw a plan for themselves, but such as we may so far come into as is requisite for the ends of peace and fellowship and communion with one another.

"I write this in haste, and not with a very clear head. Therefore I desire you to keep it only for your own information, in answer to your question how to behave yourself on such an important occasion. If need require, I will think farther of this matter, and be ready to give my judgment on any scheme the D^r shall please to communicate to me.

"You assure him that nothing he intrusts me with shall go any farther than he himselfe allows it to do. I am, with great esteem, Reverend Sir, your assured Friend

"W. Cant.

⁎ "You should show the D^r the Forms of our Consecration of Bishops and Deacons."

Of the inclosed letter to Du Pin, mentioned in the foregoing, we have only, so far as I can discover, two short fragments, preserved by Maclaine.[1] This is to be regretted. But we can discern from them that Wake was upholding the purity of the English Church in faith and discipline, and expressing a conviction that little would be found in it that Du Pin would desire to see changed :

"Aut ego vehementer fallor, aut in ea pauca admodum sunt, quæ vel tu immutanda velles . . . . Sincere judica, quid in hac nostra Ecclesia invenias, quod jure damnari debeat, aut nos atra hæreticorum, vel etiam schismaticorum, nota inurere."

Again, referring to the disputes about the Constitution *Unigenitus*, he forecasts the opportunities that may thence arise :

"Si exhinc aliquid amplius elici possit ad unionem nobiscum ecclesiasticam ineundam ; unde forte nova quædam reformatio exoriatur, in quam non solum ex Protestantibus optimi quique, verum etiam pars magna ecclesiarum Communionis Romano-Catholicæ una nobiscum conveniant."

Du Pin sent a courteous reply on April 6th to the Archbishop's letter, applauding his sentiments, and the style in which they were expressed ; and forwarded at the same time for Wake's acceptance, a newly-published volume of his *Bibliothèque :*

"Il est de mon deuoir de vous rendre de tres humbles actions de graces de la belle & obligeante lettre, dont votre Excellence m'a bien voulu honorer. Je n y ai pas moins admiré la beauté du style que les sentimens élevés et dignes d'un grand Prélat. Tout y respire l'amour de la paix, la douceur, la moderation, la charité Chrétienne ; en un mot l'esprit de l'Euangile. Il n y a que les éloges que vous

[1] P. 147.

m' y donnés,[1] que je regarde comme vn effet de votre pure bonté, sachant combien je les merite peu. J'ai remis entre les mains de Mr de Beauuoir vn exemplaire de mon premier Tome de la *Bibliotheque des auteurs Ecclesiastiques séparés de la communion Romaine*.[2] Je vous prie dagréer ce petit temoignage de ma reconnoissance, & d'être persuadé que je suis auec un tres profond respect,

"Monseigneur,
"De Votre Excellence
"Le tres humble & tres obeissant seruiteur
"Du Pin docteur de Sorbonne.
"à Paris le vi auril 1718."[3]

So far the correspondence had not gone beyond mutual expressions of goodwill. But an event presently occurred which tended to bring matters to a head. This was the delivery by De Girardin of an address to the Doctors of the Sorbonne, at a special meeting called on March 28th, 1718. After encouraging them to proceed with a plan which had been formed for drawing a line of distinction between the essentials and non-essentials of the faith, he added, that such a course would satisfy the members of the English Church that they did not hold all papal decisions to be articles of faith. The English Church, he said, moreover, might be more easily reconciled to them than the Greek. The very dissensions existing between themselves and the Roman Court would at least dispel the fear of papal domination with which the English were possessed, and would make their return to the bosom of the Church a speedier matter than their separation in former times had been. The oration in full is as follows:[4]

"Venerande Domine Decane,
Vosque Patres sapientissimi,
Etsi nihil est quod Ego adjiciam tot Eruditissimorum hominum sententiis, liceat tamen per vos, Patres sapientissimi, quæ sentio

---

[1] Either for "avez donnés" or "donnez."
[2] See note above, p. 49.
[3] *Wake Corresp.*, cclviii., No. 66.
[4] *Wake Corresp.*, cclviii., No. 67. A short extract from it is given by Maclaine, p. 148.

breviter eloqui; ne aut doctoris parùm esse functus officio, aut patriam videar deseruisse : quorum alterutrum aut esset naturæ contrarium, aut religioni, si minus noxium, at certe in hoc tam illustri Doctorum cœtu non honorificum nec gloriosum.

"Sacra Facultas Parisiensis fidei suæ fundamentis ad capita quædam revocandis, atque in unum volumen redigendis, hactenus idcirco allaboravit, ut et quam profiteatur ipsa religionem aperiret, et populo veritatem inter erroremque fluctuanti, quod tutè sequatur ex instituti pietate monstraret.

"Quo igitur, cum sibi præstanda proposuerit sacer ordo, et doctis fidem probare suam et indoctis sanæ doctrinæ facem præferre; huic duplici muneri, meo quidem judicio, non satisfaciet rectius, quam si scriptis suis ipsam theologiæ mandaverit medullam, neglecto cortice, id est, intempestivarum quæstiuncularum farragine, in qua nonulli, quibus id suppetit otii scilicet, operosè nugantur. Quid quod metus est, ne leviores quædam rei ecclesiasticæ leges, quibus potest ad Ecclesiæ arbitrium derogari, cujusmodi sunt diversa Liturgiarum idiomata, intentio Ministri, casus reservati, cœlibatus—et alia quamplurima, quæ prudens prætereo—metus inquam est ne ipsis fidei dogmatibus a plerisque accenseantur; cum, omnibus his in unum librum promiscue congestis, imperitum vulgus unum etiam eundemque honorem habendum esse plerumque existimet.

"Huic malo si volueritis occurrere, Patres sapientissimi, omnes singulosque doctrinæ vestræ articulos novæ incudi refingendos poliendosque committetis, præscindite quicquid redundat, quidquid præcipuum atque adeo rei cardo est, breviter dilucidèque exponite. Hac via Christianæ gregis disciplinæ non consultetis modo, sed et Fratribus nostris, infelicissimarum insularum incolis, excutietis tenebras, quarum delusi caligine dictitant nobis pro fidei dogmate haberi quidquid vel in rebus levissimis summo Pontifici, quidquid Ecclesiæ etiam ad tempus servari placuerit.

"Opinionem hanc ex eorum animis evellite : sternite viam, qua gentes, non tam sua quam aliena culpa transfugæ, ad nostra possint remeare castra. Nostis enimvero luctuosum Brittanniæ fatum; nec vos latet eam, ex quo est ab Ecclesiæ parentis avulsa corpore, velut ramus ab arbore abscissus, non suo sed adulterino succo ita nutriri, ut infinita propemodum produxerit hæreseōn genera, Deo æquè ac sibi ipsis pugnantia.

"Posset tamen exortum inter utramque Ecclesiam dissidium vobis arbitris componi, et gratia ab aliquot annis intermissa denuo iniri feliciterque redintegrari. Est quidem ingens malum, sed non insanabile. Maximæ sunt occursuræ difficultates, sed vobis dignissimæ. Qui enim fontes, olim puri atque illimes, malesana Principum iniquitate, in impuras a recto cursu voragines sunt detorti, ii jam antiquos quærant alveos, in oceanum unde fluxerunt vobis deducentibus redituri: imo crediderim Anglos in Ecclesiæ consortium comunionemque reduci posse facilius quam olim Græci sunt reducti; et, ut hic negotii minus, ita plus utilitatis et gloriæ, futurum.

"Per eam igitur scientiæ gloriam, quam estis toto terrarum orbe consecuti; per eam flagrantissimam charitatem, cujus pio ardore accensi ad extremos hominum Jappones,[1] propagandæ religionis studio convolatis; per majestatem sanctitatemque doctrinæ Christianæ, cujus vos constantissimi semper præcones, sæpe etiam defensores vel cum vitæ periculo extitistis acerrimi; concipite animis, et aggredimini tam pulchrum opus. Habetis in hoc augustissimo doctorum cœtu legiones fortissimorum pugilum, qui prælientur prælia Domini. Facient profecto offensiones, quæ vos inter et senatum Capitolinum videntur intervenisse, ut Angli, deposito servitutis metu, in Ecclesiæ gremium revolent alacrius quam olim inde, quorumdam exosi tirannidem, avolarunt. Meministis ortas Paulum inter et Barnabam dissensiones animorum eo tandem recidisse, ut singuli propagandæ in diversis regionibus fidei felicius insudarint sigillatim quam junctis viribus fortasse insudassent.

Itaque, Patres sapientissimi, *induite vos, sicut electi Dei, sancti et dilecti, viscera misericordiæ*:[2] *super omnia autem Charitatem habete, quod est vinculum perfectionis,*[3] comunionis, et consortii: *plantate et rigate; Deus autem incrementum dabit.*[4]

---

[1] Girardin may be alluding to the achievements of Xavier, the friend of Ignatius Loyola, deservedly one of the glories of the Jesuit order. It was in 1547 that his meeting with the Japanese Anger took place, which resulted in the first Christian missions to Japan. At the time when Girardin spoke, the missions of the Jesuits to China had been much more in the public mind. It was about the year 1700 that the subject of the "Chinese Ceremonies" was hotly debated in the French Church. The Jesuit missionaries, it was asserted, had compounded for success in the apparent number of conversions, by allowing many heathen rites and practices to remain unchallenged. Hence, perhaps, Girardin prefers to name Japan as a scene of missionary enterprise rather than China. See Kurtz: *Hist. of the Christian Church*, ed. 1881, ii. 173.

[2] Col. iii. 12.   [3] *Ib.* v. 14.   [4] 1 Cor. iii. 6.

"*Deus noster refugium et virtus,*[1] *qui regis Israel, qui deducis velut ovem Ioseph,*[2] *qui avertisti captivitatem Iacob,*[3] *respice in testamentum tuum,*[4] *et animas pauperum tuorum ne derelinquas in finem.*[5] *Exurge, Domine; judica causam tuam,*[6] *et ne obliviscaris voces quærentium te.*[7] *Excita potentiam tuam, et veni, ut salves populum tuum.*[8] *Ecce nunc tempus acceptabile:*[9] *conturbatæ sunt gentes, et inclinata sunt regna.*[10] *Domine Deus virtutum, Pater misericordiarum, et Deus totius consolationis,*[11] *usquequo irasceris super orationem populi tui.*[12] *Posuisti nos in contradictionem vicinis nostris, et inimici nostri subsannaverunt nos.*[13] *Deus virtutum convertere:*[14] *ne memineris iniquitatum nostrarum antiquarum:*[15] *ne reminiscaris delicta nostra, vel parentum nostrorum. Respice de cælo, et vide et visita vineam istam et perfice eam, quam plantavit dextera tua.*[16] *Cito anticipent nos misericordiæ tuæ.*[17] *Reduc captivatem nostram de cunctis locis, et lætabuntur omnes qui sperant in te: in æternum exultabunt, et habitabis in eis.*[18]

"Prononcé en sorbonne le 17 de mars, 1718, dans une
"assemblée extraordinaire de la faculté
"par Piers de Girardin
"Docteur en theologie de la
"Faculté de Paris."

A copy of the address was sent by its author to Wake, along with the following letter, dated April 30th, 1718. He mentions in the course of it that he had seen the Archbishop's letter to Du Pin, as had also Cardinal de Noailles. To be a fellow-worker in the great work of promoting peace and concord among Christians, he declares that he esteems a great privilege. Nor are the flames of dissension between the Gallican Church and the English so fierce that they cannot be extinguished.

[1] Ps. xlv. 1.
[2] Ps. lxxix. 1.
[3] Ps. lxxxiv. 2.
[4] Ps. lxxiii. 20.
[5] Ps. lxxiii. 19.
[6] Ps. lxxiii. 22.
[7] Ps. lxxiii. 23.
[8] Ps. lxxix. 3.
[9] 2 Cor. vi. 2.
[10] Ps. xlv. 7.
[11] 2 Cor. i. 3.
[12] Ps. lxxix. 5.
[13] Ps. lxxix. 7.
[14] Ps. lxxix. 15.
[15] Ps. lxxviii. 8.
[16] Ps. lxxix. 15, 16.
[17] Ps. lxxviii. 8.
[18] Ps. v. 12.

"Illustrissimo ac Reverendissimo Domino
Domino Guilielmo Wake, Cantuariensi
Archiepiscopo, Brittanniarum Primati,

Patricius Piers de Girardin, Presbyter, sacræ facultatis Parisiensis theologiæ Doctor, S. P. D.

"Quam ad Dominum du Pin scripsisti Epistolam, eam ego ita legi non semel, ut, si nomen non prætulisset tuum, e stili tamen dignitate, sententiarum gravitate et pietate, rerumque difficillimarum compendiosa facilique dilucidatione, certo colligerem, aut a doctissimo Præsule esse exaratam, aut qui exarasset esse principe mitra quam dignissimum.

"Senserunt hoc idem viri probi, præsertim eminentissimus Noalfius; qui utrum animi perspicaciam, an mansuetudinem charitatemque in scribendo tuam magis suspexerit, difficile judicium est. Expressisti enim calamo, quam pectore geris pacem, concordiæ studium, et Christianæ charitatis dilectionem, quam Christus Dominus quo suis imperavit enixius, eo nos, progenies degener, videmus impensius aversari.

"Hanc ego concordiam, et redintegrandam cum Ecclesia Anglicana fidei religionisque societatem, cum in Concione Sorbonica extra ordinem nuper indicta suasissem fusius, protulit litteras tuas Dominus du Pin, mihique legendas obtulit, ratus se non posse mihi gratulari magis, quam si ostendisset, quod dixerim, litterarum etiam tuarum auctoritate fulciri.

"Quare cum summo mihi honori esse ducerem, in eandem cum tanto tamque illustri Præsule sententiam, quasi dedita opera, conspirasse, statui habitam tunc temporis a me qualemcunque orationem tuæ Celsitudini offerendam; non quia dignam arbitror quæ tuis manibus alio nomine teratur, quam quod conciliandæ Christianos inter paci voluntatumque consensioni a me fuit consecrata. Neque enim discordiæ fax nos inter et ecclesiam Anglicanam ita videtur esse accensa, ut non possit opera atque pietate Præsulum tui similium feliciter extingui: immo si quo cœpisti pede perrexeris ipse, non dubito quin susceptum quodamodo a Celsitudine Tua et cum laude inchoatum opus gloriose sis absoluturus.

"Non deerunt qui tanti ducis auspiciis strenue rem gerunt. Conscribunt tuæ Celsitudini turmas imprimis Dominus du Pin et siqui sunt veræ religionis asseclæ. His accedet dominus de Beauvoir, cujus ea est industria, quæ tuæ in promovenda re Christiana pietati et famulari gestiat, et possit cum laude fructuque subvenire.

"Precor Deum Optimum Maximum ut Celsitudinem tuam, religionis bono, diu servet incolumem.

"Datum Parisiis pridie Calendas Maii, An. 1718."[1]

It might have been thought that the matter was now in a fair way of progress, having been discussed in the Sorbonne with no sign of disapproval. A letter received a little while before from Du Pin, also enclosing a copy of his friend's address, would strengthen such an impression. But Wake was of too cautious a disposition to form any sanguine expectations from a momentary success. He wrote to Beauvoir on April 15th, 1718, expressing his conviction that neither the Cardinal nor the Regent would go so far as to break with Rome.[2]

Du Pin, however, did not let the matter rest, and in the summer of 1718 drew up a tentative scheme, showing on what bases of agreement the two Churches might be re-united, to which he gave the name of a *Commonitorium*, or paper of instructions.[3] On August 18th, Beauvoir writes to the Archbishop that he has at last got a copy of Du Pin's *Commonitorium* and letter for his Grace. "'Tis fear'd," he says, "Cardinal de Noailles is at the bottom no friend to an Union; and perhaps it had been better if the Procureur-général Jolly had not as yet been inform'd with the design in hand."[4] To this the Archbishop replied at some length, on August 30th, 1718:

"I told you in one of my last how little I expected from the present pretences of such a union with us. Since I received the papers you sent me, I am more convinced I was not mistaken. My task is pretty hard, and I scarce know how to manage my selfe in this matter. To go any farther than I have done, even as a divine only of the Church of England, may meet with censure; and as Archbishop of Canterbury I cannot treat with those Gentlemen.

[1] *Wake Corresp.*, cclviii., No. 65.
[2] *D'un Projet*, etc., p. 4.
[3] The word is used in Ammianus Marcellinus in this sense:—"Commonitorium cum Augusti litteris tradidit." Lib. xxviii. c. 1.
[4] *Wake Corresp.*, cclxii., No. 2. On the back of this is the rough draft of the Archbishop's reply, as given in the text. The crossings out and interlineations show that the writer felt it necessary to be careful in what he wrote.

"I do not think my character[1] at all inferior to that of an Archbishop of Paris: on the contrary, without lessening[2] the authority and dignity of the Church of England, I must say that it is in some respects superior. If the Cardinal were in earnest for such a union, it would not be below him to treat with me himselfe about it. I should then have a sufficient ground to consult with my Brethren, and to ask his Majestie's leave to correspond with him concerning it. But to go any farther with these Gentlemen will only expose me to the censure of doing what in my station I ought not without the King's knowledge; and it would be very odd for me to have an authoritative commission to treat with those, who have no manner of authority to treat with me. However I shall venture at some answer or other to both their letters and papers, and so have done with this affair.

"I cannot tell what to say to M. du Pin. If he thinks we are to take their direction what to retain and what to give up, he is utterly mistaken. I am a friend to peace, but more to Truth; and they may depend upon it, I shall always account our Church to stand upon an equal foot with theirs; and that we are no more to receive laws from them, than we desire to impose any upon them. In short, the Church of England is free, is orthodox: she has a plenary authority within her selfe. She has no need to recur to others, to direct her what to believe or what to do; nor will we, otherwise than in a brotherly way, and with a full equality of right and power, ever consent to have any treaty with that of France. And therefore, if they mean to deal with us, they must lay down this for a foundation, that we are to deal with one another on equal terms. If, consistently with our own establishment, we can agree upon a closer union with one another, well: if not, we are as much, and upon as good grounds, a free, independent church, as they are. And for myself, as Archbishop of Canterbury, I have more power, larger privileges, and a greater authority, than any of their Archbishops; from which, by the grace of God, I will not depart, no not for the sake of a union with them.

"You see, Sir, what my sense of this matter is, and may think, perhaps, I have a little altered my mind since this affair was first set on foot. As to my desire of peace and union with all other Christian Churches, I am still the same. But with the Doctor's *Commonitorium*

---

[1] Here used in the literal sense of the word, which means a stamp or impress, and so the rank denoted thereby, as in Burns's well-known line. Comp. Rogers: *Naaman* (1642), "What Characters are in your seale will soon be seen by your wax."

[2] That is, except I lessen.

I shall never comply. The matter must be put into another method; and, whatever they think, they must alter some of their doctrines, and practices too, or a union with them can never be effected. Of this, as soon as I have a little more leisure, I will write my mind as inoffensively as I can to you, but yet freely too. If anything is to come of this matter, it will be the shortest method I can take of accomplishing it, to put them in the right way. If nothing (as I believe nothing will be done in it), 'tis good to leave you under a plain knowledge of what we think of ourselves and our Church; and to let them see that we neither need nor seek the union proposed, but for their sake as well as our own:—or rather, neither for theirs nor ours, but in order to the promotion, as far as possible, of a Catholic Communion among all the Churches of Christ.

"I have now plainly opened my mind to you. You will communicate no more of it to the two D^{rs}, but keep it as a testimony of my sincerity in this affair; and that I have no design but what is consistent both with the honour and freedom of our English Church, and with the security of that true and sound doctrine which is taught in it, and from which no considerations shall ever prevail with me to depart."[1]

This is plain speaking indeed; and the tone adopted by Wake is in striking contrast to that of some later seekers for reunion, who seem as if they could not grovel too abjectly before the Bishop of Rome. Yet his apprehension of incurring censure, even though he had gone so far short of half-way to meet the French theologians, was not unfounded. Archdeacon Blackburne, in the *Confessional*,[2] so misrepresented the Archbishop's action, as to state that this "pretended champion of the Protestant religion had set on foot a project for union with a Popish church; and that with concessions in favour of the grossest superstition and idolatry." The only excuse that can be made for this writer is, that he could not have, as we have, the actual correspondence before him. But to return. Reserving till afterwards a discussion of the

[1] The above is given, with some slight verbal alterations, by Maclaine, pp. 174-177; and a portion of it by Jervis, ii. 438. The first section of the letter has been omitted, as not bearing on the matter in hand.

[2] Pref. p. lxxvi (2nd ed.). It was, in fact, to rebut these charges, that Maclaine printed the copious extracts from the Wake correspondence which he has done.

contents of the *Commonitorium*, or of the portion of it which, unfortunately, is all that can be found, we will follow the course of events as reflected in the Letters.

On August 27th (O.S.), 1718, which would be September 7th (N.S.)—in any case subsequent to the letter last cited—Beauvoir wrote from Paris to the Archbishop. Referring to Du Pin and Girardin, he says:

"The two D^{rs} express'd their due sense of gratitude for the honour your Grace is pleas'd to do them; and desir'd me to present their duty and respects to you, my Lord. . . . Your Grace hath perfectly convinc'd me that there is little hope at this time of an Union. The state does not seem in a condition to do it, if it was design'd; and the Drs. and Divines here are as yet too full of prejudice. But a friendly correspondance may in time open insensibly their eyes, and perhaps afterwards incline the Court to shake off the yoake of Rome. These thoughts I keep to myself, and, according to your Grace's wise commands, I conceal from them."[1]

But events in Paris were now taking a turn which seemed likely, by loosening the adherence of part of the Gallican Church to Rome, to render it more inclined to an alliance, if not a reunion, with the Church of England.

On the same day as the last, August 27th, Girardin also wrote to the Archbishop, mentioning incidentally that the correspondence was known to Cardinal de Noailles, who had desired his hearty thanks to be conveyed to Wake for the manner in which he wrote. Girardin had written in the same tone of the interest taken in the matter by De Noailles, in his letter of April 30th (above, p. 56). Beauvoir, writing on September 14th, just afterwards, states that Du Pin assured him that the project had been communicated to De Noailles, "who approved of it'

What special conference with his brethren of the Sorbonne Girardin refers to in what he says of their "deliberations," I am not aware. But the modifications of ritual and doctrine he is prepared to accept are striking. The use of images;

[1] *Wake Corresp.*, cclxii., No. 3. The latter part is quoted by Jervis, ii. 438.

prayers to saints; Communion of the laity under one species only; papal supremacy; elevation of the Host—are all things which he says may be regarded as non-essential.

He is evidently disposed to think that the Procureur-général, Joly de Fleury, will be a valuable ally.

" . . . Grates igitur te dignas cum tibi solvere non sit meum, patiare quæso, Præsul illustrissime, ut eminentissimi Noallii nomine gratias agam tibi quam maximas; quem tu virum, etsi nunquam fortasse vidisti, novisti profecto, cum religionis ὑπερασπιστὴν appellas."

[Litterarum ab Archiepiscopo conscriptarum urbanitatem inde laudat, ipsiusque humanitatem, qui Doctores Sorbonicos fratrum nomine sit dignatus.]

"Hæc cum legerunt, exclamarunt a te jacta esse concordiæ fundamenta; suum quoque symbolum in tam pulchri operis partem esse conferendum. Deliberantibus unde potissimum auspicarentur, quidve in medium nunc temporis afferrent, author fui ut a sequentibus inciperent propositionibus, quæ a vobis nobisque communi fide verissimæ esse creduntur. Atque ut a charitate, quæ propria videtur esse tuæ Celsitudini virtus, exordiar, illud pro præcipuo atque adeo fundamentali principio statuendum est:—

" 1°. Charitas Christiana postulat, ut quæ sunt ἀδιάφορα, quæque in utramque partem salva fide possunt agitari (quemadmodum fusius doctiusque habetur in Commonitorio eruditissimi du Pin), ea non æquo modo sed et fraterno vicissim animo feramus, ne mutuæ dilectionis inter nos interturbetur commercium.

" 2°. Non peccat qui Deum adorat, nulla præsente Numinis imagine.

" 3°. Unicuique Christiano liberum est, nullo prius implorato sanctorum patrocinio Deum ipsum precari.

" 4°. Nemo duxerit nefas esse, intermissam a pluribus sæculis Laicorum sub duabus speciebus communionem redintegrari.

" 5°. Sacrosancta Episcoporum potestas a"Deo solo, salva tamen ut aiunt subordinatione, proficiscitur.

" 6°. Denique, ad sacram σύναξιν sacratissimamque Eucharistiæ mensam accedere possunt fideles, sine prævia, ut aiunt, hujus sacramenti elevatione.

"His recte et ut par est utrinque perpensis stabilitisque propositionibus, non video quomodo pacis ineundæ obices sublati esse non intelligantur. Et stabilientur illæ quidem, unionisque in nos vinculum eo stringetur facilius, quo crebriores ad nos invicem litteras ultro citroque hunc in finem miserimus . . . .

"Habemus hic virum divinitus oblatum, D. B. de joly de fleury,[1] Procuratorem regium, qui ut est loco et dignitate spectabilis, ita huic promovendo negotio utilem præstare poterit operam, et pie certe quidem volet . . . .

"Dat. Parisiis, sexto Kal. Septembr. S.N."[2]

Ever since the appeal of the four bishops, in March of the previous year,[3] party spirit had been growing more dangerous and threatening in the Gallican Church. The Sorbonne had applauded their action; the Inquisition at Rome had condemned it. A weak head swayed the destinies of the Church in Paris; one indifferent to all religion swayed the destinies of the State. The opportunity for decided action was thus presented to the Pope, and he availed himself of it. On August 28th, 1718, he promulgated the Bull *Pastoralis Officii*, in which those who had refused submission to the Constitution *Unigenitus* were pronounced no longer fit to be regarded as children of the Church, but as "disobedient, contumacious, and refractory." "Since they have departed from us and from the Roman Church," the sentence ran, "if not by express words, at least in fact, by manifold proofs of hardened obstinacy, they must be held as separated from our charity and that of the Church, and communion can no longer subsist

---

[1] M. Joly de Fleury, according to Le Roy, "Connaissait fort bien les matières ecclésiastiques, les ayant étudiées dans sa jeunesse. Il était tonsuré, quoique avocat général (lisons-nous dans les notes manuscrites d'Adrien le Page). Il se maria secrètement et conserva quelque temps ses bénéfices, sans doute pour les resigner à un de ses parents; mort depuis chanoine de Notre-Dame."—*La France et Rome*, p. 663 n. Elsewhere (p. 562) Le Roy praises his veracity; and Wake, in a subsequent letter, speaks kindly of him. Guillaume François Joly de Fleury was born November 11th, 1675, and died March 25th, 1756. His capacity for work was extraordinary. In the office of Procureur-général he succeeded D'Aguesseau, who had been made Chancellor.

[2] *Wake Corresp.*, cclviii., No. 92. The year is not given, but it must have been 1718.

[3] See above, p. 48.

between them and ourselves."[1] Let Beauvoir describe the reception which this Bull met with in Paris, and the effect it had on the schemes for comprehension.

In a memorandum, not signed, but in his writing, dated Paris, September 14th (O.S.), 1718, he notes that

"A Brief is lately come from Rome, not properly excommunicating the non-acceptants, but to separate from their communion. It was not receiv'd. However, it hath had this effect, that Cardinal de Noailles, who hitherto declined publishing his appeal, and owning it in an authentick manner, requir'd the adherence of his Chapter to this Appeal, Friday last."[2]

And in a letter to Wake, dated three days later:

"D^r Du Pin is now out of town .... I thought the *Commonitorium* very deficient, and only the opinion of a private Doctor, yet such as gave up several errors of the Romish Church. Dr Dupin assur'd me that he communicated his design to Cardinal de Noailles, who approv'd of it. But as what hath been hitherto transacted is only matter of speculation, and a charitable wish of a Christian union, it can never be look'd upon as a Treaty. I was once invited to wait upon the Cardinal, but I declin'd it; as also upon the Procureur-General.[3] I once had a conference with Dr Leger,[4] one of their most eminent Divines, and told him that all that cou'd at present be wish'd [was] that the Divines of both Churches might correspond one with another in a friendly way, to prepare matters for an Union, when God wou'd think fit to effect it. . . . The Pope's late Brief to separate from those that have not receiv'd his Constitution *Unigenitus* hath oblig'd Cardinal de Noailles to own publickly his appeal. Cardinal de Rohun[5] hath sent a mandate to his diocese,

---

[1] Jervis, ii. 239.
[2] *Wake Corresp.*, cclxii., No. 4.
[3] M. Joly de Fleury. See note above, p. 62.
[4] Described as one of the heads of the moderate Gallican party. His way of formulating the vote of the theological faculty, in the debates in the Sorbonne on the acceptance of the Constitution *Unigenitus*, was the one finally accepted. See Le Roy, p. 579. He must not be confused with Claude Leger, also a Doctor of the Sorbonne, who was Curé of Saint André-des-Arcs, Paris, in 1738.
[5] De Rohan, Bishop of Strasbourg, the great opponent of De Noailles. For a description of him see the *Mémoires* of St. Simon, vi. 417.

excommunicating all those that should appeal from the Constitution ; and so have the Cardinal de Bissi [1] and the Bishop of Evreux [2] into theirs. So that we are like to see a formal schism in France, which may induce the Appellants to seek the protection of the Church of England. I am assured that Cardinal de Noailles seems now earnest for an Union. But *that* time is to discover. But I most humbly presume that the only way for them to come to an Union is sincerely to reform their Church. For then the Union is of course made, without the formality of perhaps impracticable treaties." [3]

The likelihood of "a formal schism," as Beauvoir expresses it, must have begun to seem not wholly imaginary. As the Archbishop of Paris had appealed against the Constitution *Unigenitus*, so he now protested against the *Pastoralis Officii*, and in his protest had a large following. The Pope's patience was exhausted.[4] What the state of feeling was in Paris and in the provinces is vividly described by Beauvoir, in a letter to Wake, dated October 4th, 1718:

" . . . The Sorbonne hath appeal'd in its own name from the Pope's last letter, [and] confirm'd their adherence to the Cardinal of Noailles' mandates. The curez of Paris, Les Pères de l'Oratoire, les Carmes déchaussez, les Bénédictins de St Germain de Prez, les Augustins, the whole University, Les Chanoines de Ste Géneviève, and ceux de St Victor, have also adher'd to them. Several Bishops order'd [that] their mandates, excommunicating all those that had already, or wou'd for the future appeal, shou'd be affix'd to the gates of their palaces. But they were torn down by order of the civil Magistrates." [5]

---

[1] Henri de Thiard de Bissy, who succeeded Bossuet as Bishop of Meaux. He and Cardinal de Rohan were "les *deux oracles* de la Constitution."

[2] Le Normant: "un cuistre de la lie du peuple," as St. Simon calls him. See Le Roy, p. 514.

[3] *Wake Corresp.*, cclxii., No. 5. The latter part of this extract is quoted by Jervis, ii. 439.

[4] "Mille fois," writes Lafiteau, "je vis le Saint Père sur le point d'éclater contre quelques Parlemens. . . . Je lui représentai les dangers d'un Schisme déclaré."—*Histoire*, tom. ii., pp. 128, 129.

[5] *Wake Corresp.*, as before, No. 6.

Such being the state of things in France, the time seemed to have come, even to the cautious mind of Archbishop Wake, for reciprocating more openly the friendly advances made to him by Drs. Du Pin and De Girardin. He accordingly wrote to each of them a long and carefully-considered letter; and as the packet, being heavy, was to go with the next despatches to Lord Stair, he sent notice of it to Beauvoir in the following, dated October 8th, 1718:

"Whatever be the consequence of our corresponding with the Sorbonne Doctors about matters of religion, the present situation of our affairs plainly seems to make it necessary for us so to do. Under this apprehension I have written, though with great difficulty, two letters to your two Doctors, which I have sent to the Secretary's office, to go with the next pacquet to my Lord Stair. I beg you to enquire after them: they made up together a pretty thick pacquet, directed to you. In that to D^r Du Pin, I have, in answer to two of his MSS., described the method of making bishops in our Church. I believe he will be equally both pleased and surprised with it. I wish you could shew him the Form of Consecration, as it stands in the end of your large Common-Prayer Books.

"The rest of my letters, both to him and Dr Piers,[1] is a venture, which I know not how they will take, to convince them of the necessity of embracing the present opportunity of breaking off from the Pope, and going one step farther than they have yet done in their opinion of his authority; so as to leave him only a primacy of place and honour;[2] and that merely by ecclesiastical authority, as he was once bishop of the imperial city.

"I hope they both shew[3] you my letters: they are at this time very long, and upon a nice point. I shall be very glad if you can any way learn how they take the freedom I have used, and what they really think of it. I cannot so much trust to their answers, in which they have more room to conceal their thoughts, and seldom want[4] to

---

[1] That is, Dr. Piers de Girardin. See above, p. 47 *n*.

[2] The Archbishop's language here should be noticed. It agrees with what Pusey described as the primitive custom, "when the Bishop of Rome had a precedence of dignity, not of power."—*Eirenicon*, 1865, p. 236.

[3] The word "may" or "will" appears to be omitted.

[4] That is, "seldom fail."

overwhelm me with more compliments than I desire, or am well able to bear.

"Pray do all you can to search out their real sense of, and motions at the receipt of these two letters. I shall thereby be able the better to judge how far I may venture hereafter to offer anything to them upon the other points in difference between us: though after all I still think, if ever a reformation be made, it is the State that must govern the Church in it. But this between ourselves." [1]

The first letter in the inclosure was to Du Pin, dated October 1st, 1718. In it the Archbishop acknowledges the receipt of some manuscript treatises by him, referring in particular, we may suppose, to the *Commonitorium*; hopes that the events now taking place in Rome may induce the members of the Gallican Church to assert their rights; in England they had an example of freedom from the Papal domination; the Bishop of Rome, as having his see in what was anciently the seat of empire, had inherited a certain prerogative, but not such as to destroy the rights of kingdoms, or the standing of other bishops: let them once secure in common a state of independence of Rome, and unity in other matters, or at least freedom to differ, will be the result. As to the *Commonitorium*, he will only say for the present, that the very fact of Du Pin's considering there to be no insuperable difference between the two Churches is encouraging. If they had only full authority to confer together, a way for an honourable agreement might be discovered.

"*Spectatissimo Viro, eruditorum suæ gentis, si non et sui sæculi principi, Domino L. Ell. Du Pin, Doctori Parisiensi, Gul. prov. div. Cant. Arch^s. in omnibus* εὐφρονεῖν καὶ εὐπράττειν.[2]

"Diu est, amplissime Domine, ex quo debitor tibi factus sum ob plures tractatus MSS., quos tuo beneficio a dilecto mihi in Christo D. Beauvoir accepi. Perlegi diligenter omnes, nec sine fructu; plurima quippe ab iis cognitu dignissima vel primum didici, vel clarius intellexi: beatamque his difficillimis temporibus censeo ecclesiam Gallicanam, quæ talem sibi in promptu habeat doctorem, in dubiis

---

[1] Maclaine, p. 177.
[2] The Greek words are so written, though the compounds thus formed have, as far as I am aware, no authority.

consiliarium, in juribus suis tuendis advocatum, qui et possit et
audeat non modo contra suos vel erroneos vel perfidos symmystas
dignitatem ejus tueri, sed et ipsi summo Pontifici, ut olim B. Apos-
tolus Paulus Petro, *in faciem resistere, quia reprehensibilis est*.[1] Atque
utinam hæc quæ jam Romæ aguntur, tandem aliquando omnibus
vobis animum darent ad jura vestra penitus asserenda; ut deinceps
non ex pragmaticis, ut olim, sanctionibus, non, ut hoc fere tempore,
ex concordatis, non ex præjudicatis hominum opinionibus, res vestras
agatis; sed ea authoritate qua decet ecclesiam tam illustris ac præ-
potentis imperii, quæ nullo jure vel divino vel humano alteri olim aut
ecclesiæ aut homini subjicitur, sed ipsa jus habet intra se sua negotia
terminandi, et in omnibus, sub rege suo Christianissimo, populum
suum commissum propriis suis legibus et sanctionibus gubernandi.

"Expergiscimini itaque, viri eruditi, et quod ratio postulat nec refra-
gatur religio strenue agite. Hoc bonorum subditorum erga regem
suum officium, Christianorum erga episcopos suos, heu! nimium
extraneorum tyrannide oppressos, pietas exigit, flagitat, requirit. Ex-
cutite tandem *jugum* illud, *quod nec patres vestri, nec vos ferre potuistis*.[2]
Hic ad reformationem non prætensam,[3] sed veram, sed justam, sed
necessariam ecclesiæ nostræ primus fuit gradus. *Quæ Cæsaris erant,
Cæsari reddidimus; quæ Dei, Deo.* Coronæ imperiali regni nostri
suum suprematum, episcopatui suam ἀξίαν, ecclesiæ suam libertatem
restituit, vel eo solum nomine semper cum honore memorandus, rex
Henricus VIII. Hæc omnia sub pedibus conculcaverat idem ille
tunc nobis, qui jam vobis inimicus. Sæpius authoritas papalis intra
certos fines legibus nostris antea fuerat coercita; et iis quidem legibus,
quas si quis hodie inspiceret, impossibile ei videretur eas potuisse
aliqua vel vi vel astutia perrumpere.

"Sed idem nobis accidit quod illis, qui dæmoniacum vinculis ligare
voluere. Omnia frustra tentata; nihil perfecere inania legum repagula
contra nescio quos prætextus potestatis divinæ, nullis humanis consti-
tutionibus subditæ. Tandem defatigato regno dura necessitas sua
jura tuendi oculos omnium aperuit. Proponitur quæstio episcopis ac
clero in utriusque provinciæ synodo congregatis, an episcopus

[1] Gal. ii. 11.
[2] Acts xv. 10.
[3] In allusion to the epithet "prétendue," joined to "religion," "réforma-
tion," etc., in the language of French anti-reformers. Thus, in an ordonnance of the Regent, published in June, 1716, there was forbidden the
practice of "la religion prétendue réformée."—*La Réforme en Saintonge*,
1892, p. 105.

Romanus in Sacris Scripturis habeat aliquam majorem jurisdictionem in regno Angliæ quam quivis alius externus episcopus? In partem sanam, justam, veram utriusque concilii suffragia concurrere. Quod episcopi cum suo clero statuerant, etiam regni academiæ calculo suo approbarunt, rex cum parliamento sancivit: adeoque tandem, quod unice fieri poterat, sublata penitus potestas, quam nullæ leges, nulla jura, vel civilia vel ecclesiastica, intra debitos fines unquam poterant continere.

"En nobis promptum ac paratum exemplum, quod sequi vobis gloriosum, nec minus posteris vestris utile fuerit. Quo solo pacem absque veritatis dispendio tueri valeatis, ac irridere bruta de Vaticano fulmina; quæ jamdudum ostenditis vobis non ultra terrori esse, utpote a Sacris Scripturis edoctis quod *maledictio absque causa prolata non superveniet.* (Prov. xxvi. 2.)

"*State ergo in libertate qua Christus vos* donaverit. Frustra ad Concilium generale nunquam convocandum res vestras refertis. Frustra Decretorum vim suspendere curatis, quæ ab initio injusta, erronea ac absurda ac plane nulla erant. Non talibus subsidiis vobis opus est. Regia permissione, authoritate sua a Christo commissa, archiepiscopi et episcopi vestri in concilium nationale coeant; academiarum, cleri ac præcipue utrorumque principis, Theologicæ Facultatis Parisiensis, consilium atque auxilium sibi assumant. Sic muniti quod æquum et justum fuerit decernant; quod decreverint etiam civili authoritate firmandum curent; nec patiantur factiosos homines alio res vestras vocare, aut ad judicem appellare, qui nullam in vos authoritatem exposcere debeat, aut, si exposcat, merito a vobis recusari et poterit et debuerit.

"Ignoscas, vir πολυμαθίστατε, indignationi dicam an amori meo, si forte aliquanto ultra modum commoveri videar ab iis quæ vobis his proximis annis acciderint. Veritatem Christi omni qua possum animi devotione colo. Hanc vos tuemini: pro hac censuras pontificias subiistis, et porro ferre parati estis.

"Ille, qui se pro summo ac fere unico Christi vicario venditat, veritatem ejus sub pedibus proterit, conculcat. Justitiam veneror: ac proinde vos injuste ac plane tyrannice, si non oppressos, at petitos, at comminatos, at ideo solum non penitus obrutos, subversos, prostratos, quia Deus furori ejus obicem posuit, nec permiserit vos in ipsius manus incidere, non possum non vindicare, et contra violentum oppressorem meum qualecunque suffragium ferre.

"Jura ac libertates inclyti regni, celeberrimæ ecclesiæ, præstantissimi cleri cum honore intueor. Hæc Papa reprobat, contemnit; et dum sic alios tractat, merito se aliis castigandum, certe intra justos fines coercendum, exhibet. Si quid ei potestatis supra alios episcopos Christus commiserit, proferantur tabulæ, jus evincatur: cedere non recusamus. Si quam prærogativam ecclesiæ concilia sedis imperialis episcopo concesserint (etsi cadente imperio etiam ea prærogativa excidisse merito possit censeri), tamen, quod ad me attinet, servatis semper regnorum juribus, ecclesiarum libertatibus, episcoporum dignitate, modo in cæteris conveniatur, per me licet suo fruatur qualicunque primatu. Non ego illi locum primum, non inanem honoris titulum invideo. At in alias ecclesias dominari; episcopatum, cujus partem Christus unicuique episcopo in solidum reliquit, tantum non in solidum sibi soli vindicare; si quis ejus injustæ tyrannidi sese opposuerit, cælum ac terram in illius perniciem commovere: hæc nec nos unquam ferre potuimus, nec vos debetis. In hoc pacis fundamento si inter nos semel conveniatur, in cæteris aut idem sentiemus omnes, aut facile alii aliis dissentiendi libertatem absque pacis jactura concedemus.

"Sed abripit calamum meum nescio quis ἐνθουσιασμός, dum de vestris injuriis nimium sum solicitus: et forte liberius quam par esset de his rebus ad te scripsisse videbor.

"Ego vero uti ea omnia, quæ tu in tuo *Commonitorio* exaraveris, etiam illa in quibus ab invicem dissentimus, grato animo accipio; ita ut aperte, ut candide et absque omni fuco porro ad me scribere pergas, eaque παρρησίᾳ qua amicum cum amico agere deceat, imprimis a te peto; eo te mihi amiciorem fore existimans, quo planius quicquid censueris libere dixeris.

"Nec de *Commonitorio* tuo amplius aliquid hoc tempore reponam; in quo cum plurima placeant tum id imprimis, quod etiam tuo judicio non adeo longe ab invicem distemus, quin si de fraterna unione ineunda publica aliquando authoritate deliberari contigerit, via facile inveniri poterit[1] ad pacem inter nos stabiliendam, salva utrinque ecclesiæ catholicæ fide ac veritate.

"Quod ad alteros tuos tractatus de constitutione episcoporum in ecclesiis vacantibus, siquidem Papa legitime requisitus facultates suas personis a rege nominatis obstinate pernegaverit,[2] in iis sane reperio

---

[1] This should rather be "possit."

[2] The reference is plainly to a difficulty which had arisen in the previous year, from the refusal by the Pope of canonical institution to prelates who had been nominated to French sees. No fewer than twelve were in this predicament. "Boldly confronting the difficulty," says Jervis, "the

quod non tua eruditione et judicio sit.[1] Quare ne prorsus ἀσύμβολος discedam, ordinem tibi breviter delineabo constituendi episcopos in hac reformata nostra ecclesia.[2] Tu judicabis an aliquid magis canonice vel excogitari vel statui potuerit.[3]

The tenor of the letter to De Girardin, which forms the second inclosure, is similar to that of the other. The great point is, that the usurped authority of the Pope must be rejected. The language of Firmilianus to Pope Stephanus was applicable again. If Clement XI. has declared them to be separate, let them take him at his word. He congratulates the Gallican Church on having such men at the head of affairs as Cardinal Noailles and the Procureur-général De Fleury. With leaders like them what might not the Church in France accomplish?

"*Præstantissimo viro, consummatissimo Theologo, Domino Patricio Piers de Girardin, sacræ Facultatis Parisiensis Theologiæ Doctori, Gul. prov. div. Cant. Arch[s] gratiam, pacem et salutem in Domino.*

"Post prolixiores epistolas eruditissimo confratri tuo, Domino Doctori Du Pin, hoc ipso tempore exaratas, quasque ego paulo minus tuas quam illius existimari velim, facilius a te veniam impetrabo vir spectatissime, si aliquanto brevius ad te rescribam: et in illis quidem animi mei vel amori vel indignationi libere indulsi, eaque simplicitate, qua decet Christianum et maxime episcopum, quid vo-

---

Council of Regency appointed a commission of laymen, with the Duc de Saint Simon at its head, to inquire into the means of supplying these vacancies in the episcopate without the intervention of the Roman Pontiff. It was an enterprise which had already more than once terrified the Vatican; and in the present instance its result was eminently successful. The tidings no sooner reached Rome, than the bulls for the twelve bishoprics were dispatched with such precipitate haste, that the courier who brought them expired from the effects of fatigue on reaching Paris."—*Gallican Church*, ii. p. 239, quoting Lemontey and Picot.

[1] Something appears to be wanting here. We should perhaps read: "In iis *nihil* sane reperio quod non tua . . *dignum* sit."

[2] Unless the Archbishop's letter was prolonged beyond what Maclaine has preserved, the description here promised was meant to be supplied by Beauvoir's pointing out to Du Pin the form of consecration in the Book of Common Prayer. See the request made to him in the letter above, p. 65.

[3] Maclaine, pp. 178-183.

bis mea saltem sententia factu opus sit, aperte exposui. Si quid, vel tuo vel illius judicio, asperius quam par esset a me exciderit, cum vestri causa adeo commotus fuerim, facile id homini tam benevole erga vos animato, uti spero, condonabitis; unaque reminiscemini nullam unquam vobis stabilem inter vos pacem, aut catholicam cum aliis unionem, haberi posse, dum aliquid ultra merum honoris primatum ac προεδρίαν Pontifici Romano tribuitis.

"Hoc nos per aliquot sæcula experti sumus: vos jam sentire debetis, qui nescio quo insano ipsius beneficio adeo commodam occasionem nacti estis, non tam ab illius decretis appellandi, quam ab ipsius dominio ac potestate vos penitus subducendi. Ipse vos pro schismaticis habet, qualem vos eum censere debetis. Ipse a vestra communione se suosque separandos publice denunciat. Quid vobis in hoc casu faciendum? Liceat mihi veteris illius Cæsareæ episcopi Firmiliani verbis respondere.[1] Sic olim Stephanum Papam acriter quidem, sed non ideo minus juste, castigavit: *Vide qua imperitia reprehendere audeas eos qui contra mendacium pro veritate nituntur . . . Peccatum vero quam magnum tibi exaggerasti, quando te a tot gregibus scidisti: excidisti enim te ipsum. Noli te fallere. Siquidem ille est vere schismaticus, qui se a communione ecclesiasticæ unitatis apostatam fecerit. Dum enim putas omnes a te abstineri posse, solum te ab omnibus abstinuisti.*—Cypr. Op. Epist. 75.

"Agite ergo, viri eruditi, et quo divini providentia vocat, libenter sequimini. Clemens Papa vos abdicavit; a sua et suorum communione repulit, rejecit. Vos illius authoritati renunciate. Cathedræ Petri, quæ in omnibus catholicis ecclesiis conservatur, adhærete: etiam nostram ne refugiatis communionem; quibuscum si non in omnibus omnino doctrinæ Christianæ capitibus conveniatis, at in præcipuis, at in fundamentalibus, at in omnibus articulis fidei ad salutem necessariis, plane consentitis; etiam in cæteris, uti speramus, brevi consensuri. Nobis certe eo minus vos vel hæreticos vel schismaticos confidite, quod a Papa ejecti pro hæreticis et schismaticis Romæ æstimemini.

"Sed contrahenda vela, nec indulgendum huic meo pro vobis zelo,

---

[1] The reference is to a long letter from Firmilian, Bishop of Neo-Cæsarea, to Cyprian (Cypriani *Opp. Ep.* 75; in Fell's edition, p. 288), written, according to Bishop Fell, in A.D. 256, in which he gives utterance to severe strictures on the line of action taken by Pope Stephanus I., on the rebaptism of heretics. The genuineness of the letter, which has been attempted to be called in question, is supported by a strong consensus of MSS.

etsi sit *secundum scientiam.* *Prudentibus loquor: vos ipsi quod dico judicate.*

"Ad literas tuas, præstantissime Domine, redeo, in quibus uti tuum de mediocritate mea judicium, magis ex affectu erga me tuo quam secundum merita mea prolatum, gratanter accipio, ita in eo te nunquam falli patiar, quod me pacis ecclesiasticæ amantissimum credas, omniaque illi consequendæ danda putem, præter veritatem. Quantum ad illam promovendam tu jamjam contuleris, ex sex illis propositionibus, quas tuis inseruisti literis, gratus agnosco: ac nisi ambitiose magis quam hominem privatum deceat me facturum existimarem, etiam eruditissimis illis confratribus tuis doctoribus Sorbonicis, quibus priores meas literas communicasti, easdem per te gratias referrem. Sane facultas vestra Parisiensis ut maximum in his rebus pondus merito habere debeat, sive numerum, sive dignitatem, sive denique eruditionem suorum membrorum spectemus, ita a vobis exordium sumere debebit unio illa inter nos tantopere desiderata, siquidem eam aliquando iniri voluerit Deus.

"Interim gratulor vobis post illustrissimum Cardinalem Noaillium, alterum illum ecclesiæ catholicæ, fidei catholicæ, columnam et ornamentum, procuratorem regium D.D. Joly de Fleury;[1] quem virum ego non jam primum ex tuis literis debito prosequi honore didici, verum etiam ob ea quæ vestri causa his proximis annis publice egerit, antea suspicere et pene venerari consueveram. Sub his ducibus, quid non sperandum in publicum vestrum ac catholicæ ecclesiæ commodum? Intonet de Vaticano Pontifex Romanus, fremant inter vos ipsos conjurata turba, Romanæ curiæ servi magis quam suæ Galliæ fideles subditi. His præsidiis ab eorum injuriis tuti vanas eorum iras contemnere valeatis.

"Ego vero, uti omnia vobis publice fausta ac felicia precor, ita tibi, spectatissime vir, me semper addictissimum fore promitto. De quo quicquid alias senseris, id saltem ut de me credas jure postulo: me sincere veritatem Christi et amare et quærere, et, nisi omnino me fallat animus, etiam assecutum esse. Nulli Christiano inimicus antehac aut fui aut deinceps sum futurus. Sic de erroribus eorum, qui a me dissident, judico, ut semper errantes Deo judicandos relinquam. Homo sum; errare possum. Sic vero animatus audacter dicam: hæreticus esse nolo. Te vero, siquidem id permittas, fratrem; sin id minus placeat, saltem id indulgebis ut me vere et ex animo profitear, excellentissime Domine, tui amantissimum.

"W. C."[2]

[1] See note above, p. 62. [2] Maclaine, pp. 183-186.

The way in which these letters were received by Du Pin and De Girardin is notified in the following communication of Beauvoir to Wake, dated Paris, October 22nd, 1718:

"I have deliver'd your Grace's letters to the two Doctors, who think themselves highly honour'd by them . . . They are extreamly satisfy'd with the account of the succession of the English Bishops. For before they were in an errour about it. Dr Dupin had several months ago the Form of Consecration,[1] and hath it still. . . . The Sorbon hath appointed twelve Doctors to prove the truth of every Proposition, condemn'd by the Constitution *Unigenitus*, by Scripture and the writings of the Fathers. They hope that the Pope will excommunicate them by name, that they may have a better opportunity to shake off his yoake."[2]

Beauvoir further writes to the Archbishop, November 5th (O.S.), 1718:

"Your Grace's letter to Dr Dupin hath been communicated to the Cardinal de Noailles, who hath a copy of it. The Procureur-Général is also to have one, when he comes to town, and he is expected this day. 'Tis blaz'd about that there is a correspondence carry'd on still to unite the Gallican with our Church, and that this correspondence is carry'd on with your Grace. I find that the anti-constitutionists[3] industriously spread this rumour for their advantage here. Your Grace's vindication of the succession of the Bishops of the Church of English [*sic*] is allow'd by the two Doctors satisfactory."

After referring to the proceedings in the Sorbonne, Beauvoir continues:

"However, Dr D. is firm in trying to pass the fourth part,[4] which is designed to circumscribe the exorbitant power of the Pope. I conjecture, your Grace's last letter hath wrought this good effect upon him, tho' he hath not declar'd it. . . . An Archbishop, tho' trampl'd

---

[1] This refers to the request of Archbishop Wake that Beauvoir would let Du Pin see the Form in the Book of Common Prayer. See above, p. 65.
[2] *Wake Corresp.*, cclxii., No. 7.
[3] That is, those opposed to the acceptance of the Constitution *Unigenitus*.
[4] This refers to the last of the four propositions submitted to the Sorbonne, given afterwards at full by Du Pin in his letter to Wake, December 1st of this year.

upon by Rome, when tinctur'd with the purple of that Court,[1] is hardly induc'd to assert his proper rights and Priviledges."[2]

A little later De Girardin himself writes to the Archbishop. The letter is a short and somewhat mysterious one, evidently leaving more to be explained by the bearer:

"Paris, the 7th 9bre,[3] N.S. [1718].

"My Lord,

"Mr. Haris[4] the bearer has entered into the secret. Your Grace may confide in him, as far as prudence and discretion can goe. The attourney general, Mr de Joly de Fleury's absence occasions my silence. Your Grace shall hear from me next month. I leave the rest to the discretion of Mr Haris; and am, with a most profound respect and perfect veneration, My Lord,

"Your Grace's most humble and most obedient servant,
"P. Piers de Girardin."[5]

The same feeling that some secrecy was still needful shows itself in the next letter of Wake to Beauvoir. The date of it is November 6th; but as this is Old Style, it was written later than De Girardin's:

"Your last letter[6] gives me some trouble, but more curiosity. I little thought, when I wrote to your two Doctors, that my letters should have been read, much less copies of them given to any such great persons as you mention. I write in haste, as you know, and trust no amanuensis to copy for me, because I will not be liable to be

---

[1] De Noailles had been made a Cardinal in 1700. See above, p. 27.

[2] *Wake Corresp.*, cclxii., No. 8. The first part of this letter is printed by Jervis, ii. 439. The date there given, November 8th, is incorrect.

[3] That is, November.

[4] A pencilled note in the *Beauvoir Corresp.* indicates that this was Dr. John Harris, author of the *History of Kent*, and other works. He was born about 1667, educated at St. John's College, Cambridge, where he graduated B.A. in 1687; M.A. in 1691, and D.D. in 1699. About 1702 he was living in Amen Corner, in the City of London, where he taught mathematics. His *Lexicon Technicum*, 2 vols., 1708, is regarded as the progenitor of scientific encyclopædias. He died, in destitution brought on by his own imprudence, in 1719.

[5] *Wake Corresp.*, cclxii., No. 9.

[6] The one dated November 5th.—See above, p. 73.

betrayed. And upon a review of my foul[1] and only copy of them, since I had your account from Paris, I find some things might have been more accurately expressed, had I taken more time to correct my style. But I wish that may be the worst exception against them. I fear the freedom I took in exhorting them to do somewhat in earnest, upon so fair a provocation, with regard to the papal authority, though excused as well as I could, will hardly go down so effectually as I could wish with them.

"This raises my curiosity to know truly and expressly how that part of my letters operated on both your Doctors; which, by a wary observation, you may in good measure gather from their discourse. I cannot tell whether they shewed my letters to you. If they did, I am sure you will think I did not mince the matter with them in that particular.

"Of your two Doctors, Dr Piers seems the more polite. He writes elegantly both for style and matter, and has the free air, even as to the business of an union. Yet I do not despair of D^r Du Pin, whom, thirty years ago, in his collection of tracts relating to church discipline,[2] I did not think far from the kingdom of God."[3]

It is plain from what Beauvoir wrote above, that, in spite of any precautions which Wake and De Girardin might think fit to observe, the matter had begun to be publicly talked of in Paris. The services at the Chapel of the English Embassy, probably in consequence of this, were thronged by French people. Beauvoir writes to Wake, November 14th (O.S.), 1718:

"Last Sunday we had a prodigious crowd, and tho' I was oblig'd to perform in English, in duty to My Lady Stair, who was at Church, it being our English day, yet, after the English Prayers and Sermon

---

[1] We should now say a "rough" copy; but we retain the use of its opposite, "fair," in this connection.

[2] In 1686 Du Pin had published at Paris, in 4to, a volume of Latin essays, under the title: *De antiqua Ecclesiæ disciplina Dissertationes historicæ*. The general tendency of the writer may be inferred from a few entries in the Index. Under "Romanus Episcopus" we find: "Non ordinabat Patriarchas in Oriente, nec Metropolitanos in Gallia, Hispania, Africa"; "Primatum habet jure divino"; "Non habebat olim jus admittendarum appellationum in judiciis Episcoporum"; "Rejicitur ea quæ ipsi tribuitur infallibilitas"; "Eum Concilio subesse ostenditur"; "Ipsum non posse reges deponere."

[3] Maclaine, p. 186.

were over, I directed a Psalm to be sung in French, and preach'd afterwards in that language for the benefit of the numerous brethren that had not understood what I said before; and gave the Communion afterwards to about thirty persons, most from the country."[1]

Wake paid little attention to these tokens of passing excitement, and went calmly on, shaping out in his own mind the course he thought needful for the great object in view. To Beauvoir he writes, November 18th, 1718:

"Good Sir,

"Tho' I wrote to you so lately by the post, yet I cannot let Monsr d'Artis[2] go from me without taking some notice of him, and recommending him to your favour, for the little time he tarries at Paris. I do also embrace this opportunity of sending a new edition of St Clement's *Epistle* to Mr du Pin, which he will find more carefully collated with the Alexandrine MS., and more accurately set forth with all the annotations (some never before printed) of learned men upon it, than in any other edition before made of it."[3]

Then, after alluding to the addresses in the Houses of Parliament:

"But these are matters for our Politicians to consider of. They no further concern us, than as we are members of the State, as well as ministers of the Church, and ought to desire the welfare of the one no less than of the other. At present, my more particular curiositie leads me to know the sentiments of the leading men in France with regard to the Court of Rome; from which if we could once divide

---

[1] *Wake Corresp.*, cclxii., No. 10.

[2] This is probably Gabriel d'Artis, the author of a work now very rare: *La maîtresse clé du royaume des cieux, enrichie de perles du plus grand prix; ou Dissertation contre le Papisme*, published anonymously in London, without date. See Brunet's *Manuel*. D'Artis was a Protestant, and, it would seem, somewhat of a rolling stone, having been for some years a journalist in Holland, as well as pastor of a French church at Berlin. He is said to have died in London, about 1730.

[3] In the preface to the second edition of his *Genuine Epistles of the Apostolical Fathers*, 1710, Wake speaks of having carefully collated Young's edition of St. Clement's *Epistle to the Corinthians* with the Alexandrine MS. The annotations referred to in the text are the marginal notes, in which Wake had the assistance of Dr. Grabe, the editor of the Septuagint.

the Gallicane Church, a reformation in other matters would follow of course.

"The scheme that seems to me most likely to prevail is : to agree in the independence (as to all matters of authority) of every national Church on any other; of their right to determine all matters that arise within themselves; of a union with one another by circular Letters, whereby a person (for example) who is excommunicated in one Church shall not be received into communion by any other : and, for points of doctrine, to agree as far as possible in all articles of any moment (as in effect we either already do, or easily may); and for other matters to allow a difference, till God shall bring us to a union in those also. One only thing should be provided for, to purge out of the public offices of the Church all such things as hinder a perfect communion in the service of the Church; that so, whenever any come from us to them, or from them to us, we may all join together in prayer and the Holy Sacraments with each other. In our Liturgie there is nothing but what they allow of, save the single rubric relating to the Eucharist:[1] in theirs nothing but what they agree may be layd aside, and yet the public offices be never the worse or more imperfect for want of it.

"Such a scheme as this I take to be a more proper ground of peace at the beginning, than to go to more particulars. If in such a foundation we could once agree, the rest would more easily be built upon it.

"If you find occasion, and that it may be of use, you may extract

---

[1] This is the one placed at the end of the Communion Service, commonly called "the black rubric," as not being printed in red like the others. It is really not a rubric at all, but a Declaration of Council, hastily added in 1552, to explain the rubric directing Communicants to kneel. Bishop Thirlwall, who will not be suspected of excessive attachment to rites or ceremonies, condemned it in one of his Charges :—" It must be admitted," he says, " that in the Declaration or Protestation, at the end of the Communion Office, the Church of England has deviated from her own vantage-ground to that of her adversary, and has stated the question in the way most favourable to the doctrine of the Church of Rome; for it is made to turn on a purely metaphysical proposition as to the nature of 'body':—*it being against the truth of Christ's natural body to be at one time in more places than one.* This is virtually to fall into the Romish error, and to stake the truth of her doctrine on the soundness of a scholastic speculation, which, as a Church, she has no more right to deny than the Church of Rome to affirm."—See Procter : *Of the Common Prayer*, ed. 1892, p. 383 *n.*

this project, and offer it to their consideration, as what you take to be my sense in the beginning of a treaty: not that I think we shall stop here, but that, being thus far agreed, we shall the more easily go on to a greater perfection hereafter.

"I desire you to observe, as much as you can, where it is that I may the most properly write to your Doctors.[1] I took the subject of the Pope's authority in my last, as arising naturally from the present state of their affairs, and as the first thing to be settled in order to a union. How my freedom in that respect has been received, I desire you freely to communicate to, Good Sir, your assured friend,

W. Cant."[2]

Du Pin was not hasty in replying to letters. What follows is his answer, written on December 1st, 1718, to the Archbishop's of just two months before. That this was a direct reply, and that no earlier one had intervened, is obvious from the reference with which it begins to the Greek salutation in the Archbishop's letter.

Du Pin disclaims in it all merit for being an upholder of the Gallican liberties. That, he says, is the traditional principle of the Sorbonne, and had lately been stoutly maintained by his colleagues in the Faculty. He then shortly reiterates the positions they were prepared to maintain; which are, in fact, almost the theses he had propounded in his treatise *De antiqua Ecclesiæ doctrina.* I have not transcribed the whole of the letter. It is dated: "Parisiis, Kalendis Decembris, secundum stylum nostrum, anno 1718."[3]

"Illustrissime ac Reverendissime Præsul:
Quibus in Epistolæ tuæ titulo me ornas laudibus, id benignitati tuæ, non meis meritis tribuendum existimo. Quod vero mihi apprecaris εὐφρονεῖν καὶ εὐπράττειν,[4] moniti loco esse vis; idque tanto

---

[1] On December 14th, 1718, De Girardin writes to Wake, desiring him to address "à M. l'abbé Piers de Girardin, Doct^r de Sorb., vis à vis le caffé de la Providence, Rue de Betizy."—*Wake Corresp.,* cclxii., No. 15.

[2] *Beauvoir Corresp.,* No. 5. The latter part of the letter is printed by Maclaine, p. 187.

[3] *Wake Corresp.,* cclviii., No. 98.

[4] See the note above, p. 66.

auctore et auspice quantum in me erit adimplebo. Nihil est quod mihi gratuleris de suscepta sæpe sæpius a me Libertatum Ecclesiæ defensione. Hoc et olim Gersonius,[1] Richerius,[2] aliique complures majores nostri egregiè præstiterunt, et nunc Theologi omnes Galli paucis exceptis profitentur. Id sacra Facultas Theologiæ Parisiensis adversus Romanorum Pontificum vsurpationes et vltramontanorum Theologorum errores præstitit. Quid dicam quam fortiter, quam gnaviter, novissime adversus Constitutionem quæ incipit *Vnigenitus* insurrexerit. Hæc te docebunt acta appellationis ejus, quæ ni fallor D. Beauvoir ad te transmitti curavit.

"Libertates ecclesiæ Gallicanæ non sunt privilegia[3] ipsi peculiaria, sed jus antiquum, quod retinet, et quo regitur. Ad illud firmandum tendunt Pragmaticæ Sanctiones S. Ludovici, et Bituricensis conventus.[4] Has strenue tutantur et leges regni, et regum edicta, et innumera supremorum apud nos senatuum decreta.

[1] For Jehan le Charlier, commonly called, from his birthplace, Gerson, see A. L. Masson's *Jean Gerson, sa vie, son temps, ses œuvres*, 1894; and *L'esprit de Gerson*, par E. le Noble de Tenneliere, 1801. The great Chancellor was born at Gerson, a little hamlet, no longer existing, in the parish of Barby, about four or five miles from Réthel. He was the eldest of twelve children of poor parents; born December 14th, 1363; died July 12th, 1429. His work in upholding the independence of the Gallican Church, and in healing the schism in the Papacy, by getting the Council of Pisa convened, is too well known to need mention.

[2] Edmond Richer was born September 30th, 1560, at Chaource, or Chource, a little village in the diocese of Langres, and studied at the Sorbonne, of which he became doctor in 1590, and in 1608 was elected Syndic of the Faculty of Divinity. His publishing works of Gerson, and (in 1611) his *Libellus de Ecclesiastica et Politica Potestate*, drew upon him the ill-will of the Ultramontane party. He was deprived of his office in the Sorbonne, and afterwards imprisoned. He died November 28th, 1630 (according to other accounts, 1631), and was buried in the Chapel of the Sorbonne. A portrait of him is prefixed to the *Libellus* before mentioned, a work which, in spite of its name, fills two closely-printed quarto volumes. See *La Vie d'Edmond Richer, docteur de Sorbonne*, par Adrien Baillet, 1715, and Mosheim's *History*, tr. by Maclaine (ed. 1811), iv., p. 201.

[3] So le citoyen Grégoire, Bishop of Blois, when preaching in Notre Dame at the opening of the National Convention, June 29th, 1801, speaking of the rights of the Gallican Church, said: "Faut-il répéter que ce ne sont pas des privilèges? C'est le droit commun de toutes les églises."

[4] See above, p. 7.

(1.) "Si¹ Pontifex recuset electo a Rege consuetas dare litteras, jus nobis est secundum ipsa Concordata ordinationes in Gallia a Metropolitano juxta morem antiquum peragi.

(2.) "Circa causas Ecclesiasticas, quæ ex Gallia emergunt, nullæ Romæ judicantur, sed ab Episcopis regni, a quorum judiciis provocatur ad Metropolitanum.

(3.) "Quod Romani Pontificis jurisdictionem in regnum spectat, ea coercitur [sic] tam arctis limitibus, ut nihil nobis obesse possit; nec enim potest quidquam in temporalia, et in spiritualibus intra Canonum antiquorum regulas continetur.

(4). "Primatum ejus, id est, inter Episcopos primum tenere locum, ut tota antiquitas affirmat, et ipsi Græci (licet a Romana ecclesia diuulsi) fatentur, agnoscimus. Sed primatus ille non ei dat superiorem gradum inter Episcopos: eorum tantum coepiscopus est, licet inter Episcopos primus."

The extract which follows was thought by Dr. Pusey to be of special interest to the readers of his *Eirenicon*,² "as illustrating how earnest the good old man was in his love for peace and union, and on what terms he thought it might be effected." It shall therefore be given in his version:

"In these days³ I have read the book of William Forbes,⁴ Bishop of Edinburgh, entitled *Considerationes modestæ et pacificæ Controversiarum*, etc., London, 1658. The Bishop seems to be of the same mind as you and I; for the whole subject of the work turns on

¹ In this and the following sections are the four propositions referred to by Beauvoir in his letter to Wake (see above, p. 73). For clearness, I have prefixed the numbers to them.

² Ed. 1865, p. 235.

³ Too literal a rendering of the Latin idiom for "within the last few days," or "lately."

⁴ William Forbes, born 1585, died 1634, was the first Bishop of Edinburgh, the see having been almost created for him, so high did he stand in the estimation of Charles I. His principles made him obnoxious to the Scottish Presbyterians; but all admitted that he was a men of great learning and piety. In his *Bibliothèque des auteurs séparez de la Communion de l'Eglise Romaine*, tom. ii. (1719), pp. 583-591, Du Pin analyses the opinions advanced in Forbes's *Considerationes*, quoted in the text, and adds that "ce livre peut être très utile pour contribuer à la réunion de l'Eglise Anglicane avec la Romaine." See also the article by the Rev. James Cooper in the *Dict. of National Biography*.

this, to show that the controversies between us may easily be settled, if only the fairer Theologians are heard on both sides, if dictating is avoided, and we are led, not by party spirit, but by love of seeking the truth.¹ The posthumous works of Lancelot [Bishop Andrewes], published A.D. 1629, aim at the same end.² I propose to transcribe from these and other works of the like sort, and from those of the more peace-loving on our side, testimonies to each Article, side by side, and to send them to you."

From the beginning of the next letter, it would seem that Beauvoir had found some opportunity of carrying out the Archbishop's desire, and submitting his "project" to the consideration of his friends at the Sorbonne. But both began to feel that, unless more decided counsels prevailed, little progress would be made. The indecision of Cardinal de Noailles, above all, was fatal. That "honnête pusillanime," as Le Roy calls him, had been threatened by the Regent with the terrors of the Canon law, if he held out longer against the wishes of the

---

¹ In the Latin : "Ut ostendat facile conciliari posse eas quæ sunt inter nos controversias, si modo æquiores audiantur, ab injuriis abstineatur, nec partium studio sed quærendæ tantum veritatis amore ducamur."
With this may well be compared the closing words of a contemporary writer, Sir Peter King, who, towards the end of his *Enquiry* (1713), says, in a kindred spirit :—" Our disputes are only about lesser matters, about modes and forms, about gestures and postures, and such like inferior matters ; about which it should grieve a wise man to quarrel ; *and which with the greatest ease in the world might be composed and settled, if managed by men of prudence and moderation.*"

² The xcvi *Sermons* of Bishop Andrewes (b. 1555, d. 1626) were not published till after his death, when, by the King's command, they were edited by Bishop Laud and J. Buckeridge. But Du Pin may be rather thinking of the *Opuscula quædam posthuma*, which were published in 1629 ; especially as in the *Bibliothèque des auteurs separez*, ii., p. 593, he says of Andrewes : " Il avoit encore fait plusieurs discours sur differens sujets importans, prononcez et écrits en Anglois, *qui ont été traduits en Latin*, et imprimez après sa mort à Londres en 1629." Du Pin was evidently impressed by the learning and moderation of the Bishop of Winchester. He concludes his account of him with the words : " Il étoit bon Theologien, parloit sagement et méthodiquement, étoit fort modéré dans ses sentimens, et plus ennemi des Calvinistes que des Catholiques Romains. Son style est simple, mais mâle, et tel qu'il convient à un Docteur en Théologie et à un Evêque."

Pope in the matter of the *Pastoralis Officii* ;[1] and he had bent before the storm. As the safest way of extricating himself, he had, about this time, resigned his seat in the Council of Conscience.[2] A less hopeful tone is now perceptible in the letters of the English correspondents. The following, of Wake to Beauvoir, is dated December 2nd, *Old Style*, 1718, and may therefore possibly be later than Beauvoir's next, the date of which is not so described :

"I am glad the two Doctors seem to receive my last letters so well. The truth is that, while they manage as they do with the Court of Rome, nothing will be done to any purpose, and all ends in trifling at the last. We honestly deny the Pope any authority over us. They pretend, in words, to allow him as much as is consistent with what they call their Gallican privileges: but, let him ever so little use it contrary to their good liking, they protest against it, appeal to a general council, and then mind him as little as we can do.

"In earnest, I think we treat his Holiness not only with more sincerity, but more respect than they. For to own a power, and yet keep a reserve to obey that power only so far and in such cases as we make ourselves judges of, is a greater affront, than honestly to confess that we deny the power, and for that reason refuse to obey it. But my design was partly to bring them to this, and partly to see how they would bear at least the proposal of totally breaking off from the Court and Bishop of Rome.

"What you can observe or discover more of their inclinations in this particular will be of good use ; especially if it could be found out what the Court would do, and how far that may be likely to countenance the clergy in such a separation. In the mean time, it cannot be amiss to cultivate a friendship with the leading men of that side, who may in time be made use of to the good work of reforming in earnest the Gallican Church. I am a little unhappy that I have none here I yet dare trust with what I do ; though I am satisfied most of our high-church bishops and clergy would readily come into such a design. But these are not men either to be confided in, or made use of, by your assured friend

"W. Cant."

"P.S. Did Cardinal de Noailles know what authority the Archbishop

---

[1] Lafiteau, ii. 129. See also above, p. 62.   [2] Jervis, ii. 240.

of Canterbury has gotten by the Reformation, and how much greater a man he is now than when he was the Pope's *Legatus natus*,[1] it might encourage him to follow so good a pattern, and be assured, in that case, he would lose nothing by sending back his cardinal's cap to Rome. I doubt your Doctors know little of these matters."[2]

Beauvoir writes in much the same strain, December 9th, 1718:

"They labour under great difficulties, which yet with God's blessing may easily be overcome. It is as clear as the day, that, unless they honestly and without prevarication assert broadly the authority of their Church, they'll labour still under as great inconvenience as formerly, and that the Court of Rome will be at last too hard for them, and contrive heavyer chains to load them with, when a fit occasion offers."[3]

What Wake had said about "having none here whom he yet dare trust with what he did," is incidentally confirmed by what Dr. Harris writes to Beauvoir. Harris, it will be remembered, was the bearer of a letter from De Girardin to the Archbishop.[4]

"Dec. 11th 1718. Soho Square.
" . . . I visited lately the Arch-Bishop of Canterbury, with a letter from Dr Pierce:[5] who made a very honourable mention of you, and make no doubt has it in his heart to find some recompence suitable to so ancient and considerable a merit as yours.[6] I had some discourse with his Grace upon the affairs of the Sorbonne, to which he is disposed to concur with his utmost assistance; though as yet

---

[1] A *Legatus natus* was a legate not specially appointed (*legatus datus*), but *ex officio*. According to Walcott, the Archbishop of Canterbury was the Pope's *Legatus natus* from 1195 till the Reformation. "The one relic of this office is his power of giving Lambeth degrees."—*Sacred Archæology*, 1868, p. 347.

[2] Maclaine, pp. 188-189.

[3] Jervis, ii. 439.

[4] See above, p. 74.

[5] That is, Dr. Piers de Girardin.

[6] Though I have not thought it necessary to trouble the reader with them, it is only fair to add, as completing a true picture, that many of Beauvoir's letters to the Archbishop contain reminders of his claim to some preferment.

he has communicated no part of that great and valuable design to any of his brethren the Bishops, finding, as I'm afraid, some indispositions at home; which, like deformities in a fair body, 'tis our prudence to hide, and throw a mantle over them as decently as we can."[1]

So far as there was any necessity for reserve, Wake appears to have succeeded better in keeping his proceedings unnoticed in England, than his correspondents had done in France.

"The business of the Union of the two Churches," writes Beauvoir to him on the last day of the year, "hath made a noise both here and at Rome."

And again, on the 14th of February following:

"All the town rings of an Union, and many declare openly that they wish it." "I could wish," he adds in the previous letter, "that Mr. Barbe, chaplain to the Dutch ambassador, had not given Cardinal de Noailles and the curez of Paris grounds to be dissatisfied. He hath acted with a great deal of zeal, but did not consider he was in Paris."[2]

We may perhaps infer from this, that curiosity about a leading topic of the day in Paris had impelled numbers to attend the chapels of the embassies of the Protestant states, and that the chaplain at the Hôtel d'Hollande had either indiscreetly encouraged this, or had brought into prominence topics on which he and the English chaplain would not be at one.

Writing on February 11th, 1719, Beauvoir mentions that "the women put in prison for going to the Dutch ambassador's chappel are intirely oblig'd to my Lord Stair for their inlargement."[3] Even a year later he speaks of "seven Protestants imprison'd the day before, coming from his Excellency's Chappel." "They threaten," he adds, "to suffer no French to resort to our Congregations, and to place Guards within

---

[1] *Beauvoir Corresp.*, No. 6.
[2] *Wake Corresp.*, cclxii., Nos. 15, 17.
[3] *Ib.*, No. 16.

twenty paces of our Hotel, to take up those that come to it upon Sundays."[1]

Whatever interest these details might have for the Archbishop, he did not suffer his attention to be diverted by them from the main actors. Writing to Beauvoir, January 23rd (O.S.), 1718-19, he says:

"When you see my letter (for I conclude the Doctor will shew it you),[2] you may do well to bring on the discourse of our episcopal rights and privileges in England; and particularly of the prerogatives of the Archbishop of Canterbury, which I believe are greater than those of the Archbishop of Rheims, or of all the Archbishops in France. This may raise in them a curiosity to know more of this matter: which if they desire, I will take the first little leisure I have to give them a more particular account of it.

"We must deal with men in their own way, if we mean to do any good with them. They have been used to a pompous ministry; and, like the Jews heretofore, would despise the Messiah himself, if he should come in a poor and low estate to them. And therefore, though, for myself, I account all temporal grandeur as nothing, and am afraid it has rather hurt the Church of Christ, and the true spirit of piety and religion, than done any real service to either; yet it may be the means of disposing these gentlemen to a more favourable thought of and inclination towards a reformation, to convince them that they may return to the truth of Christianity, and leave the corruptions of Rome, without losing any honour, any power, that a servant of Christ would desire to be troubled withal.

"Had the first reformers in France yielded to this scheme, as we in England shewed them an example, the whole Gallican Church had come in to them, and been at this day as we are now. We must therefore hit off the blot which they made, and satisfy their ambition

---

[1] *Wake Corresp., ib.*, No. 77, dated February 3rd, 1719-20. The numbers attending may be inferred from his mention of "about 210 communicants" the Sunday week before; and again, under date May 19th, 1719, "I gave four times last week the Communion privately, and last Sunday to above 150 persons. We had about 400 hearers. The Dutch about 800, and 400 communion [*sic*], and yesterday about 150." *Ib.*, No. 30.

[2] The letter referred to is probably the inclosure in one dated January 18th, spoken of in the next of February 5th. If so, it does not appear to have been preserved.

so far as to shew them that they may reform, without giving up either their authority or revenues, and be still as great, but much better, bishops, under our circumstances than under their own.

"As to the Pope's authority, I take the difference to be only this: that we may all agree, without troubling ourselves with the reason, to allow him a primacy of order in the episcopal college. They would have it thought necessary to hold communion with him, and allow him a little canonical authority over them, as long as he will leave them to prescribe the bounds of it. We fairly say[1] we know of no authority he has in our realm. But, for actual submission to him, they as little mind it as we do.

"At present he has put them out of his communion.[2] We have withdrawn ourselves from his. Both are out of communion with him; and I think it is not material on which side the breach lies."[3]

The publicity, which the correspondence between Du Pin and the English Archbishop was rapidly gaining, now compelled the French government to interfere. De Noailles, when questioned on the subject, would give no definite answer; and so an order was given to seize the letters and papers connected with it in the possession of Du Pin. The date of the order, as we learn from Lafiteau, was February 10th. The proceedings described by Beauvoir, in a letter written two days earlier, must, therefore, have been only preliminary. His use of initials for the names of the Abbé du Bois and others, suggests an affectation of mystery.

"Paris, 8th Feb'y 1719, (S. N.)[4]

"My Lord,

"I flatter myself that Your Grace hath receiv'd D'r Dup's letter, and the Books sent by M'r Smith, and likewise those directed to M'r Vaillant.

"Since I have acquainted you, My Lord, that the Procur'r Gnll sent for D'r D—— to have exact account of his correspondance in England, Mons'r l' abbé du B—— by the Regent's order summon'd

---

[1] That is, "say outright."
[2] By the Bull *Pastoralis Officii*. See above, p. 62.
[3] Maclaine, pp. 190-191.
[4] *Wake Corresp.*, cclviii., No. 110.

him to appear at his Hotel, and seem'd satisfy'd with what had been transacted therein; but desir'd he might see the original letters the D^r hath received, which the D^r hath transmitted. Monsr l'abbé du B—— spoke with due respect and veneration of Your Grace. Some of the chief of the Sorbon have intreated Lord Stair to wait upon M^r L'abbé du B. to state this matter right, fearing Dr Dup—— might have made some mistake. For it is perceiv'd his unweary'd labours have very much impair'd him.

"D^r P—— hath been several times to wait upon Mr L'a. du B——, and hath even writ to him to shew what steps have been made for an Union. Some people believ'd that Dr P. would soon be sent for, if the Court was angry, and that my Lord Stair wou'd speak to me about that affair. But neither hath Dr P. been cited nor spoken to. Which makes some friends believe that the *Puissances* are not displeas'd, and that those who wish the peace and concord of all Christian Churches need not despair."

Then follows an account of the prodigious crowds at Lord Stair's public entry into Paris on the preceding Sunday, and of the writer himself, as chaplain, "in a silk gown and cassock of Ráá [1] de St Maur."

"The Dutch ambassador's Chaplain's zeal hath hurt those people. Last Sunday sennight six women were carry'd to Prison, coming from the Dutch ambassador's House. One is relas'd, because she is a Genevois's wife, but the others are still in prison. . . . . ."

As the Jesuit Father Lafiteau was present at the Palais-royal when Du Pin's papers were brought in for examination, it will be interesting to compare his account of the matter with Beauvoir's.

"Autre entreprise," he writes,[2] "que j'aurois eu de la peine à croire, si je n'en avois vu les Actes originaux, c'étoit le projet d'unir le Parti des Oposans à l'Église Anglicane. Le Docteur Dupin, si connu en Sorbonne par ses excès,[3] en avoit fait un Traité entier. Il

---

[1] "Ras de Saint-Maur" was a kind of silk stuff, the name being formed like "Ras de Saint-Lô," "Ras de Châlons." St. Maur was noted for its mulberry trees. Why Beauvoir should spell the word "Ráá," I cannot tell.

[2] *Histoire*, ii., pp. 138-139.

[3] This description of the "good old man," as Pusey calls him, shows to what lengths party-spirit will go. In a *Lettre adressée à l'Auteur de la*

y avoit long-tems qu'on le sçavoit dans une étroite liaison et dans une rélation continuelle avec M^r l'Archevêque de Cantorbéry, c'est à dire, avec l'homme que l'Église Anglicane a de plus distingué par le rang. D'abord on suposa que ce commerce de lettres étoit un devoir de pure civilité. Dans la suite on y soupçonna du mistère. Il en transpira quelque chose. On y eut l'œil. Enfin, on parvint à la connoissance du plus abominable complot qu'un Docteur Catholique ait pû trâmer en matière de Religion. L'Apostasie n'eut jamais rien de plus criminel."

This "abominable complot!" Such is the language used on one side. But let Lafiteau continue:

"Le 10 Février l'ordre fut donné en ma présence, d'aller chez le Sieur Dupin et de saisir les papiers.[1] Sur l'heure ils furent tous enlevés. Je me trouvai au Palais Royal au moment qu'on les y aporta. Il y étoit dit, que les principes de notre Foi peuvent s'accorder avec les principes de la Religion Anglicane. On y avançoit que, sans altérer l'integrité du Dogme, on peut abolir la Confession auriculaire, et ne plus parler de *Transubstantiation* dans le Sacrement de l'Eucharistie, anéantir les Vœux de Religion, permettre le Mariage des Prêtres, retrancher le Jeûne et l'Abstinence du Carême, se passer du Pape, et n'avoir plus ni commerce avec lui, ni égard pour ses Décisions."

Waiving for the present the question whether the summary of doctrines here given as held by Du Pin is correct, we shall now be able to follow the Archbishop better in what he writes to Beauvoir on February 5th (that is, 16th in New Style), 1719:

"I do not doubt that mine of the 18th of January, with the two

---

nouvelle Rélation de ce qui s'est passé dans les assemblées de Sorbonne, au sujet de l'enregistrement de la Bulle Vnigenitus, 1716, Du Pin had to defend himself from charges of personal violence more suggestive of modern electioneering proceedings than of a meeting of "grave and reverend signiors." "Fausseté," No. xxiii., which he rebuts, was that "Monsieur Du Pin s'avança vers M. Humbelot, en lui montrant le poing, pour l'empêcher de passer outre et d'aller du Bureau." "Ce fait," Du Pin shortly observes, "est absolument faux."—P. 134.

[1] In the article on Wake in the *Biographia Britannica*, Girardin is said to have been the one whose papers were seized. The mistake is repeated in Chalmers's *Biographical Dictionary*.

inclosed for my Lord Stair and Dʳ Du Pin, are before this come safe to you. I should not be sorry if, upon this late transaction between the Doctor and the ministry, you have kept it in your hands, and not delivered it to him. I had just begun a letter to Dʳ Piers, but have thrown aside what I writ of it, since I received your last; and must beg the favour of you to make my excuse to him, with the tenders of my hearty service, till I see a little more what the meaning of this present inquisition is.

"I am not so unacquainted with the finesse of courts, as not to apprehend that what is now done may be as well in favour of the Doctor's attempt, as against it. If the Procureur-general be indeed well affected to it, he might take this method, not only to his own security, but to bring the affair under a deliberation, and give a handle to those whom it chiefly concerns, to discover[1] their sentiments of it. But the matter may be also put to another use, and nobody can answer that it shall not be so; and till I see what is the meaning of this sudden turn, I shall write no more letters for the French ministry to examine, but content myself to have done enough already to men who cannot keep their own counsel, and live in a country where even the private correspondence of learned men with one another must be brought to a public enquiry, and be made the subject of a state inquisition.

"I am not aware that in any of my letters there is one line that can give a just offence to the Court. I always took it for granted, that no step should be taken towards an union, but with the knowledge and approbation, and even by the authority, of civil powers; and indeed, if I am in the right, that nothing can be done to any purpose in this case but by throwing off the Pope's authority, as the first step to be made in order to it, it is impossible for any such attempt to be made by any power less than the King's. All therefore that has passed hitherto stands clear of any just exception as to the civil magistrate: it is only a consultation, in order to find out a way how an union might be made, if a fit occasion should hereafter be offered for the doing of it.

"Yet still I do not like to have my letters exposed in such a manner, though satisfied there is nothing to be excepted against in them; and think I shall be kind to the Doctors themselves to suspend, at least for a while, my farther troubling of them. I hope you will endeavour,

---

[1] That is, for them to *uncover*, or disclose, their sentiments. Comp. Psalm xxix. 9.

by some or other of your friends, to find out the meaning of this motion: from whom it came, how far it has gone, what was the occasion of it, and what is like to be the consequence of it; what the Abbé du Bois says of my letters, and how they are received by him and the other ministers. I shall soon discover whether any notice has been taken of it to our ministry; and I should think, if the Abbé spoke to your Lord about it, he would acquaint you with it."[1]

In reply to the request for information here made, Beauvoir wrote on February 11th, telling the Archbishop that "the Cardinals of Rohan and Bissi complain'd, in a memorial to the Regent, that Cardinal de Noailles was inducing the Sorbonne to join with the Church of England, and withdraw from the Church of Rome; and had employ'd D^r Du Pin to manage that affair, and a correspondence with your Grace."[2]

The news did not surprise the Archbishop.

"I do not at all wonder," he writes to Beauvoir, February 24th, 1718-19, "that the Cardinals Rohan and Bissi should do all they can to blacken the good Cardinal De Noailles, and in him the party of the Anti-Constitutionists; but especially the Sorbonne, their most weighty and learned adversaries: and I am sensible that such a complaint is not only the most proper to do this, but to put the Court itself under some difficulties, which way soever it acts upon it. But I am still the more curious to learn, if it were possible, not only the proceedings of the Ministry above-board hereupon, but their private thoughts and opinions about it. I am under no concern upon my own account, farther than that I would be unwilling to have my letters scanned by so many great men, which will scarcely bear the judgment of my very friends.

"You must do me the favour to get out of your Doctors, what will be most obliging to them; whether to continue to write to them, or to be silent for a while, till we see what will be the effect of this enquiry.

"In the mean time it grows every day plainer, what I said from the beginning, that no reformation can be made but by the authority and with the concurrence of the court; and that all we divines have to

---

[1] Maclaine, pp. 191-193.
[2] *Wake Corresp.*, cclxii., No. 16.

do is to use our interest to gain them to it, and to have a plan ready to offer to them, if they would be prevailed upon to come into it.

"I am at present engaged in two or three other transactions of moment to the foreign protestants, which take up abundance of my time. God knows what will be the effect of it. Nevertheless, if I can in any way help to promote this, though I am at present without any help, alone, in this project, I shall do my utmost, both to keep up my poor little interest with the two Doctors and their friends, and to concert proper methods with them about it. The surest way will be, to begin as well, and to go as far, as we can, in settling a friendly correspondence one with another; to agree to own each other as true brethren, and members of the Catholic Christian Church; to agree to communicate in every thing we can with one another: which on their side is very easy, there being nothing in our offices in any degree contrary to their own principles; and, would they purge out of theirs what is contrary to ours, we might join in the public service with them, and yet leave one another in the free liberty of believing transubstantiation or not, so long as we did not require anything to be done by either in pursuance of that opinion.

"The Lutherans do this very thing. Many of them communicate not only in prayers but the Communion with us; and we never enquire whether they believe consubstantiation, or even pay any worship to Christ as present with the elements, so long as their outward actions are the same with our own, and they give no offence to any with their opinions.

"P.S.—Since this last accident, and the public noise of an union in Paris, I have spoken something more of it to my friends here; who, I begin to hope, will fall in with it. I own a correspondence, but say not a tittle how far, or in what way, I have proceeded, more than that letters have passed, which can no longer be a secret. I have never shewn one of my own or the Doctors' to anybody."[1]

The "transactions of moment to the foreign protestants," to which the Archbishop alludes in this letter, were probably the efforts made, in which he took an active part, to obtain toleration for Protestants abroad, especially in Hungary and Piedmont.

As far back as 1699,[2] when preaching on a Fast-Day at

---

[1] Maclaine, pp. 193-195.
[2] The Sermon was published the same year. See also above, p. 47.

St. James's, Westminster, he had publicly pleaded the cause of the suffering Vaudois. His interest in them, and in other persecuted adherents of the reformed faith abroad, never slackened. In consequence, he was looked up to with widespread affection and respect by Protestant communities on the Continent. This feeling showed itself strikingly on his appointment to the Archbishopric in 1716, when letters of congratulation poured in upon him from Poland, Geneva, and many other parts.[1] What he had specially in his thoughts, when writing as above to Beauvoir, was no doubt an application, in which he had got the prime minister, Lord Sunderland, to join him, to interest the King on behalf of suffering Protestants in the dominions of the Emperor and the King of Sardinia. In a Latin letter to the ministers and professors at Geneva, dated April 8th, 1719, Wake expresses a confident hope that George I. may have already instructed his ambassadors to those powers to use their influence for gaining the desired toleration.[2]

An event was now fast approaching, which, more perhaps than any other single thing, brought the negotiations with the Doctors of the Sorbonne to a fruitless end. This was the death of Du Pin. He was not yet quite sixty-two years old, having been born in June, 1657. But laborious study had aged him beyond his years ; and the trouble and disgrace into which he had fallen, by having his papers seized, may well have

[1] See vol. cclviii. of the *Wake Corresp.*, which is largely filled with letters of this description. No. 15,521 of the Additional MSS. in the British Museum also contains a letter of his on behalf of the Reformed Churches of Poland and Transylvania.

[2] The letter is given at full in Maclaine, pp. 201-205. The way in which the Archbishop of Canterbury was looked up to as a friend and patron by foreign Protestants, at this time, comes out incidentally in the life of Antoine Court. Speaking of his efforts to satisfy those who had opposed the *Assemblées*, he says : "J'écrivis, par leur ordre, une lettre à l'archevêque de Cantorbéry, qui contenoit un détail abrégé des églises sous la croix, et que milord archevêque présenta au Roy, qui en parut touché et promit sa protection à nos églises. Sa Majesté ne tarda pas de nous en donner quelque marque."—*Mémoires d'Antoine Court*, 1885, p. 194.

preyed on his mind. Beauvoir, writing to the Archbishop, April 13th (O.S.), 1719, while able to inform him that the persecution of the Reformed in Paris was abated, and that "many, God be praised, were added to the Church of England from popery," has to admit that "the business of an union is suspended. Dr Dupin and Dr Piers appear very easy about that matter. The first visibly decays, and the other hath much abated of his courage."[1]

The news, as might be supposed, was painful to the Archbishop to receive. He writes to Beauvoir on April 29th:[2]

"I am much concerned to hear that D^r Du Pin decays so fast: I fear'd by his last letter that he was sinking. Pray, is there any good print of him taken these last years? for I have one that was made when he was a young man.

"I am sorry Dr Piers grows faint-hearted. I never thought anything could be done as to a reformation in France without the authority of the court; but I was in hopes the Regent and others might have found their account in such an attempt; and then the good disposition of the bishops, clergy, and Sorbonne, with the Parliament of Paris, would have given a good deal of spirit and expedition to it.

"I have done what was proper for me in that matter. I can now go no farther, till the abbot Du-Bois[3] is better disposed. Yet I shall still be pleased to keep up a little esteem between those gentlemen, which will do us some good, if it does not do them any service. I am apt to think the good old man does not think us far from the kingdom of heaven.

"I have with this sent a letter of friendship to Dr Piers, which you will be so kind as to send him, with my kind respects."

To Du Pin himself, Wake addressed the following touching letter. It is dated May 1st, 1719, but from some unexplained delay was not sent in time to reach Du Pin before his death on June 6th. On that account it was returned to the writer, who,

---

[1] *Wake Corresp.*, cclxii., No. 25.
[2] Maclaine, who quotes the letter (p. 196), gives the year as 1718, but it should undoubtedly be 1719.
[3] For this would-be Richelieu, see Jervis, ii. 242-44.

however, allowed Beauvoir first to take a copy of it. It is this copy that is here reproduced : [1]

"Præstantissime Domine, Frater in Christo colendissime,

"Quanto mærore ultimæ tuæ literæ animum meum affecerint, nescio quibus verbis pro amore in te meo satis exprimere valeam. Etsi enim nihil in se novi accidisse putandum sit, cum audiamus hominem fragilem languescere, infirmum ægrotare, etiam mortalem mori; est tamen aliquid in amicitia, quod in his quæ animum concernunt ægre se rationi submittat, nec absque gravi mentis contentione patitur ut ea in illis facile perferamus, quæ in aliis vulgaria, nec sapientis viri æstimatione digna esse putaremus.

"Ego sane jam sexagenario major,[2] sanitatis toto vitæ meæ tempore dubiæ ac plerumque infirmæ, morbis atque doloribus assuetus, sæpe in confinio mortis positus, etiam nunc ex nupero accessu Cholico plurimum debilitatus, neque adhuc ad pristinas vires restitutus, minime omnium ad hæc appropinquantis ultimi hujusce vitæ termini præsagia et quasi præludia perturbari debeo. Et tamen, quamvis hæc quotidie experior, in his exerceor, ad hæc animum meum quantum fieri potest compono, quæ mea est vel propria infirmitas, vel in amicos affectus, non possum non in illis lugere, quod in se adeo non dolendum scio, ut potius optandum esse judicem. Tibi certe tali viro mors minime invidenda; cujus ut spes, corona, merces est in cælo, ita tum demum perfecte beatus es futurus, ubi ab hac terrena corporis mole liberata anima tua in cælum recipietur.

"Speraveram equidem tua auctoritate, constantia, eruditione, pietate, moderatione, quæ omnia adeo in te perfecta esse noscuntur ut vix in aliis singula, præclaré aliquid ad Dei gloriam ecclesiæque Gallicanæ utilitatem perfici potuisse. Crediderim advenisse tempus in quo, excusso Romanæ tyrannidis jugo, una nobiscum in eandem communionem coalesceretis.

"In dogmatibus, prout a te candide proponuntur, non admodum dissentimus; in regimine ecclesiastico minus; in fundamentalibus, sive doctrinam sive disciplinam spectemus, vix omnino. Quam facilis erat ab his initiis ad concordiam progressus, modo animos haberemus ad pacem compositos. Sed hoc principibus seculi non arridet, unionis

---

[1] *Beauvoir Corresp.*, No. 8. A portion of it (from *speraveram* to *amplectamur*) was printed by Maclaine, p. 197.

[2] Wake was born in the same year as Du Pin, but survived him nearly eighteen years. His faculties had failed him some time before his death. See Cole's *Collections*, vol. xl., p. 21 (Additional MSS., No. 5,841).

inimicis etiam plurimum displicet: neque nobis forte dabit Deus esse tam felicibus, ut ad hujusmodi unionem nostram qualemcunque operam conferamus. Relinquamus hoc Illi, in cujus manu sunt rerum omnium tempora et occasiones. Sufficiat voluisse aliquid in tam insigni opere; forte et semina in terram projecisse, quæ fructum tandem multiplicem proferant. Interim, quod nemo nobis denegare possit, nos invicem ut fratres, ut ejusdem mysticè corporis membra, amplectamur. Amemus non vulgari illo amore, quo alii solebant, quibus non affulsit Evangelii lux, sed ea charitate quam relligio nostra docuit, cujusque umbram tantum philosophi olim in suo etiam arctissimo amicitiæ exercitio nobis exhibuerunt.

"Ipse vero Deus pacis et amoris utrumque [e] nobis in sua et Ecclesiæ suæ pace atque unitate conservet in hoc sæculo, et ad *cælestem suam Hierusalem, civitatem Dei viventis, ecclesiam primitivorum qui conscripti sunt in cælis*,[1] perducat in futuro. Ibi nulla erit sapientibus hujus mundi autoritas, nulla illis potentia, quorum omnis est in ore religio, ad cor raro descendit. Ibi omnes passiones, omnia præjudicia, paci ac concordiæ inimica, penitus ex animis nostris eximentur. Idem sentiemus, idem quæremus omnes. Illuc jam oculis mentis prospiciamus per fidem ambulantis non per speciem. Illinc animum illum cælestem derivemus, qui etiam in beatis illis sedibus nobiscum permanebit, nosque ad accessum in beatas illas oras præparabit.

"Ego pro te, frater dignissime, non desinam orare, ut hunc in se[2] animum magis magisque efficere dignetur S. Dei Spiritus. Tu pro me interpella ad Thronum Gratiæ, ut eandem in me mentem efformare velit; utque mortali hac vita, quod brevi fiet ab utroque peracta, amicitia nostra, sero hic nimis inchoata, in cælis permaneat, vigeat, augeatur, perficiatur. In hoc voto desinit, vir clarissime, tuus in Domino frater, omni officio conjunctissimus,

"W. Cant."

("*Ex ædibus nostris Lambethanis, I° die Maii,* A.D. 1719.
À monsieur, Monsieur du Pin, Docteur de la Sorbonne et Professeur de Theologie à Paris.")

Having been deprived of his papers, Du Pin would naturally wish to leave behind him some account of his correspondence

---

[1] Heb. xii. 23.

[2] If *se* be right, the sense will be: "this disposition towards Him" (the Holy Spirit). But it may be a slip of the pen for *te:* "this disposition in you."

with the English Archbishop, which might represent his conduct in a true light for posterity. Such a one he drew up, so far as his strength would allow, and intrusted it to Beauvoir for transmission to the Archbishop. For certain reasons, Beauvoir considered the account defective, and kept it back till the defects could be supplied. The letter, dated Paris, May 19th (O.S.), 1719, in which he relates this, is further interesting as showing the difficulties besetting the attempt to make the principles of the English Church a *via media* between Gallicanism and Protestant nonconformity:

". . . D^r Du Pin put into my hands an account of his correspondence with England, to be communicated; but I have stop'd it, and kept, as finding it deficient; and when rectify'd to be convey'd to your Grace for approbation, before it appears to anybody else. That G.[1] Man grows very weak every ways. Age and hard labour hath worn him out.

"The minds of the Clergy seem more and more averse to the Papal power; yet, intoxicated with their former prejudices, they can't yet bear the thought that he should only be *Primus inter pares.* For they would allow him some sort of authority over all the Church; as that of seeing the Canons put in execution, &c., with a sort of jurisdiction in point of discipline. They may be as yet ashamed to own, that they have so long submitted to his imaginary power. However, I observe that those I converse with are not angry that the usurpations of the Pontif of Rome should be run down and exploded, and do not decline the company of one that doth it modestly and freely.

"The Dutch chaplain,[2] tho' he hath been assur'd of the contrary,

---

[1] An abbreviation for either "great" or "good"; probably the former, as Beauvoir, writing on June 7th, speaks of "the great D^r Du Pin."

[2] I am not sure whether this person, of whom Beauvoir has complained before (p. 87) was named Horner. If so, he was himself in correspondence with Wake a few years later on. Writing on April 22nd, 1722, he describes the kind of service he held: "J'ay cru ne pouvoir mieux faire que de me servir de la Liturgie que M. Osterwald a composé, puisqu'il l'a tiré [sic] en partie de celle d'Angleterre . . . . ayant vu que ce peuple aime la lecture de la Parole de Dieu, de même que les Pseaumes en vers, mais qu'il a pour ainsi dire une plus haute opinion des Sermons que de la pure Parole de Dieu." On the 29th of the same month he expresses to Wake his regret that the enforcement of the *Consensus* on the Vaudois

persists to affirm that no reform'd foreign minister is admitted to receive ordination in the Church of England, unless he owns his former ordination null.[1] This notion hath given great offence, and made a vast many of these people doubt whether we are of the same religion. And what confirms them in their opinion is that I do not allow their ministers, that preach in my Lord Stair's Chappell, to make use of our Liturgy, or to help me at the Communion; but only to say the Lord's Prayer before Sermon; and that after their Sermon I conclude and give the Blessing.

"If I am in the wrong, I beg pardon and further instructions from your Grace. It would very much reconcile the minds of the Protestants here to the Church of England, if foreign ministers were allow'd to officiate among us, and I to officiate among them. This would remove an unhappy stumbling-block, which is industriously put in our way. I can by no means believe I have authority to remove it; and therefore I earnestly intreat your Grace's commands in this particular, that I may govern myself accordingly."[2]

What Beauvoir's objections were to the first draft of the *Relation* will be seen more clearly from a letter written by him to the Archbishop, when over in England a few months later:

"Clapham, 24th July, 1719.

"My Lord,

"About the beginning of May last, D^r Du Pin, designing to communicate to a very great man [3] the enclosed Relation, written by

---

"n'arrête tout court la Reunion, que vous avez si bien avancée."—*Wake Corresp.*, cclxii., Nos. 27, 29.

[1] The difficulty, if it is one, seems to solve itself. The applying for ordination would in itself be an admission that ordination had not previously been received. There appear, however, to have been occasional instances in which persons who found obstacles in the way of their being ordained to the pastorate of reformed communities abroad, came over to England, to seek for orders there. See the *Correspondance fraternelle de l'Église Anglicane avec les autres Églises Réformées*, par Claude Groteste de la Mothe, ministre de l'Église de la Savoye, 1705, p. 99. From this scarce little book, and its sequel, *Entretiens sur la Correspondance*, 1707, much light is gained on the relation between the Church of England and foreign Protestant Churches, in the early part of the eighteenth century.

[2] *Wake Corresp.*, cclxii., No. 30.

[3] No doubt, Cardinal de Noailles.

his usual Amanuensis, put it then into my hands, requiring my opinion. As I conceiv'd it defective, I desir'd it might be more full, by adding that your Grace's first Letter to him was an answer to one he had sent to You, my Lord, to return thanks for the honourable mention you was pleas'd to make of him in a letter dated 2 Jan^y, 1717 O.S., wherewith I was honour'd, to express his desire of an union between the Church of England and that of France, and to beg the favour of a Correspondance.

"The D^r readily promis'd to supply that defect, but was prevented by Death; and therefore his Relation remains as he first composa'd it.

"I most humbly beg your Blessing to,
"My Lord, your Grace's
"most humble and most obedient servant,
"Wm. Beauvoir." [2]

The draft of the *Relation* itself, composed, as Beauvoir says about the beginning of May, is as follows. It has all the appearance of being left unfinished.

"*Relation*
De ce qui s'est passé entre Monsieur
Du Pin et M^r L'archeveque de Cantorbery
au sujet des lettres qu'ils se sont mutuellement écrites.

"En 1717 L'archevêque de Cantorbery fit l'honneur à M^r l'abbé du Pin de lui écrire une lettre obligeante de complimens, et lui marqua en meme tems qu'il souhateroit que l'eglise Anglicane fût reunie avec l'eglise Gallicane. Mr du Pin répondit à cette lettre avec le respec dû à vne personne de cette consideration, et lui marqua en meme tem que nous n'etions pas si eloignés que nous ne pussions nous reunir qu'il y avait plusieurs articles, dont nous convenions, et qu'il y en avait d'autres, qui ne regardoient que la discipline, sur les quels il n pouvoit y avoir aucune contestation de part et d'autre; et qu'à l'égard des autres articles, en petit nombre, en s'éclaircissant on pourroi convenir. L'archeveque de Cantorbery temoigna qu'il ne s'eloignoi point de cette union; au contraire, qu'il la desiroit; et envoya M^r l'abbé du Pin la confession de foi et la liturgie de l'église Anglicane. M^r Du Pin dressa sur ces pieces vn memoire contenant le

---

[1] *Wake Corresp.*, cclviii., No. 140.

articles dont on convenoit ; ceux qui etoient indifferens ; et ceux sur les quels il falloit entrer vn conference pour les éclaircir : articles qui se reduisent à peu. Il l'envoya avec vne lettre a l'archeveque de Cantorbery, qui lui fit vne response, dans la quelle, sans entrer dans le détail des articles, il justifioit la succession des Archeveques et eveques d'Angleterre, dont M. du Pin sembloit avoir douté.

"Depuis ce tems la il y a eu commerce de lettres entre l'archeveque de Cantorbery et Mr du Pin, dans l'esprit de paix et d'vnion. En france des esprits malins ont regardé cela comme vne negociation préjudiciable aux interets de l'église catholique, et en ont fait courir divers bruits très faux. Cela a meme été jusqu'aux oreilles de M^r le Régent, qui a ordonne a M^r l'Abbé du Bois de prendre connoissance de l'affaire.

"Au reste, M^r l'archeveque de Cantorbery et M^r Du Pin ont toujours regardé cela comme vn projet qui ne pouvoit s'executer sans l'autorité des Puissances souveraines.[1] Monseigneur le Cardinal de Noailles, ni Monsieur le Procurateur General du Parlement de Paris, n'y sont point entrez ; mais M^r l'abbé du Pin leur a communiqué ses lettres et ses réponses. Si ce projet pouvoit reussir, il en reviendroit vn grand bien aux deux Églises, qui se soutiendroient mutuellement."

On Tuesday, June 6th, 1719, Du Pin died. Beauvoir, writing the day after, sends the intelligence to the Archbishop:

"The great Dr Dupin dy'd Tuesday last, as he had liv'd, pen in hand for the instruction of mankind and the good of the Christian Church : which might prove an irreparable loss, if Dr. Petitpied[2] did not again appear in the world, and likely to be the leading man of Sorbon. A man fit to carry on the great work of Union, and, as I am inform'd, inclin'd to do it."[4]

---

[1] In a letter written to Wake on January 13th of this year, 1719, Du Pin had expressed the same conviction :—" Ex iis aliisque meis [literis] intelligere potes quantum mihi cordi sit Ecclesiarum pax et concordia. Utinam ejus ineundæ via quædam certa affulgeret : quod fieri, vt arbitror, nequaquam potest, *nisi consentientibus sæculi potestatibus et Regnorum episcopis*. Ad hoc allabora : ego pro meo modulo (nam quis sum ?) in id etiam incumbam."—*Wake Corresp.*, cclviii., No. 99.

[2] *Wake Corresp.*, cclviii., No. 139.
[3] See the note above, p. 29.
[4] *Wake Corresp.*, cclxii., No. 31.

Again, writing to Wake on June 24th (N.S. = 13th, O.S.) 1719, Beauvoir says:

"I have joyfully made use of the liberty you condescended, m' Lord, to give, to open Dr Dupin's letter,[1] and have shew'd it t(D^r P[iers], who is very earnest to have a copy: but I will no presume to give it without leave. I most humbly beg I may b allow'd to take one for myself. I am labouring to get an exac catalogue of Dr Dupin's writtings, and one of the two pictures c him in Paris, drawn from the life.[2] . . . I do not hear of any projec to print any account of &c. If any body can do it, it is D^r P[iers] who will make no steps without a proper approbation."[3]

With the death of Du Pin, the interest of the correspond ence in which Wake was engaged practically ceases. What ever prospect of success the project of reunion may have ha in his lifetime, it was now, at any rate, at an end. De Girardi seems to have been content with a friendly disposition toward it. Petitpied, according to Lafiteau, had taken the law int his own hands, and established at Asnières, the suburba village where he was allowed to reside, a form of Divin Service after his own devising, of which that writer give a minute description.[4] Dr. Lambert, Dr. Léger, and othei of known Gallican principles, were chafing under the yok of ultramontanism; but there was no leader forthcoming t concert any plan of action with Wake. A few more lettei may be added, chiefly as showing the unsettled condition (the Church in France, before the curtain falls on this act (the drama.

The first, from De Girardin to Wake, dated August 16tl 1719, gives a lively picture of the state of feeling in th Sorbonne:

"Vendredy dernier, M. de Mesmes,[5] premier Président du Parl

---

[1] See above, p. 94.
[2] This was agreeable to the request in Wake's letter of April 29 (above, p. 93).
[3] *Wake Corresp.*, cclxii., No. 32.
[4] *Histoire*, ii. 151.
[5] Jean Antoine de Mesmes was born in Paris, November 18th, 166

ment de Paris, manda Messrs. les Doien et Syndic de la Faculté, avec d'autres Docteurs, pour leur annoncer, tant de la part de M. le Duc Régent, que de celle du Parlement, qu'on s'étoit apperçû que les Professeurs et les Bacheliers de la licence-courante[1] paroissoient affecter de ne plus soûtenir les prérogatives et les libertéz de l'Église-gallicane; que M. le Régent, et tout ce qu'il y a de bons François dans le Roiaume en étoient très indignés; et qu', en un mot, on eut a changer incessamment de conduite, si on vouloit éviter d'encourir l'indignation de la Cour.[2]

"'Comment voulez-vous, Monseigneur, que nous soûtenions les Libertéz de l'Église, répliqua M. le Doien, puisqu' on nous a dépouillés de notre propre liberté? On nous force, le pied sur la gorge, d'enregistrer la déclaration du Roy, qui défend expressément de *toucher de près ni de loin, directement ni indirectement*, les matières contestées et renfermées dans la Constitution[3]—bulle aussi étenduë que toute la Théologie ensemble; et on s'étonne, après cela, que nous paroissions abandonner la doctrine de l'Église-gallicane! En vérité, Monseigneur, ajouta le bon vieillard, l'irrégularité de la conduite, qu'on nous a forcé de tenir, fait bien sentir l'injustice du reproche qu'on nous a fait.'

"'Les intentions de la Cour, répartit M. le premier Président, ne tendoient qu' à procurer la paix de l'Église, et non à detourner le cours ordinaire de la saine doctrine. Ainsi, Messieurs, continua-t-il, on m'a chargé de vous dire que vous alliez le même train, et que

---

and educated for the law. He was Deputy Procureur-général in 1679 and President of Parliament, January 5th, 1712. He opposed the elevation of Dubois to the Archbishopric of Cambrai. He died August 23rd, 1723. See the *Biographie Universelle*.

[1] That is, those who were completing the two years' probation before being admitted to the degree of D.D. "*Licence* en Sorbonne," says a writer in Buisson's *Dictionnaire de Pédagogie*, "est un temps de deux années, que les Bacheliers passent à assister aux actes, et a y disputer, pour se mettre en état d'être reçus Docteurs."

[2] "The Court had now inclined to the side of the 'Constitutionnaires'; and upon the strength of this change of policy, the accepting bishops fulminated mandement after mandement, insisting upon absolute submission to the *Unigenitus*."—Jervis, ii. 241.

[3] This was by way of enforcing the decree of the Inquisition, obtained in the present year (1719), in which the faithful were forbidden "to print, read, or possess" the Constitution, under pain of being *ipso facto* excommunicated.

vous teniez la même route que vous avez tenuë avant l'arrivée de la Constitution. On vous prie, néansmoins, poursuivit-t-il, de ne point *attaquer de front* les propositions de cette Bulle, afin que vous ne paroissiez pas vouloir rompre-en-visière avec sa Sainteté : et il suffit pour cet effet, ajouta-t-il, que la sterilité de la langue Latine ne soit pas si grande, pour qu'on ne puisse pas s'exprimer en d'autres termes.'"[1]

"Après quoi il renvoia l'assemblée, fort satisfaite de son entretien, et du sujet de son *veniat*."[2]

Early in the following year, February 3rd, 1719-20, Beauvoir writes to Wake, reporting the result of some further efforts he had made :

"I have had at last some frequent opportunities of seeing Dr Piers, who appears zealous still for healing the divisions in the Church. Mr Lullin is not only zealous, but very capable of promoting the great work. Dr Quinant, ex-syndic about two years ago, seems inclined to write to your Grace. He is a very leading man, a good head, and full of expedients; but, as he hath shifted twice, deserves perhaps more to be manag'd than trusted. Dr Hideux's[3] great reputation in his Faculty makes him more considerable than his present abilities, which are much decay'd by age. Dr Jollin, the present syndic, who hath succeeded Dr Hideux, is [a] man of wit, and loves too much his own ease to run the least risq. However he is a stanch Jans[enist].

"The Sorbon hath done nothing of late worth mentioning. Last Monday Dr Piers was to introduce me to Dr Petitpied; but I cou'd not go, because my Lord Stair had commanded my attendance about seven Protestants, imprison'd the day before, coming from his Excellency's Chappel.[4] They threaten to suffer no French to resort to our congregations, and to place guards within twenty paces of our Hotel, to take up those that come to it upon Sundays. The Com-

---

[1] *Wake Corresp.*, cclxii., No. 37.

[2] A legal term, defined in the dictionaries as "ordre donné par le juge supérieur à un juge inférieur de se présenter en personne, pour rendre compte de sa conduite."

[3] Hideux was curé of Saints-Innocents in Paris. See Le Roy, p. 108. He took the same side as Du Pin and Petitpied in the debates on the *Cas de Conscience*.

[4] See above, p. 84.

munion was administer'd last Sunday was sennight, and we had about 210 Communicants. The Dutch chappel us'd also to be full twice on Sunday mornings; but this unexpected blow will slacken people's zeal, and keep them within doors."[1]

To this period seems to belong an undated note of De Girardin's to Beauvoir, inviting him to meet at dinner some of the persons mentioned in the preceding letter, and there to discuss a matter, the nature of which is indicated somewhat mysteriously:

"Savez-vous bien, cher ami, qu'il me tarde d'avoir l'honneur de vous voir. J'ay lieu d'espérer que vous ne manquerez point de vous trouver demain, Samedy 27°, à midy-precis, chez M. l'Abbé Quinot, où nous devons dîner avec Messrs. Lullin, le syndic, Hideux, etc. Si vous êtes engagé ailleurs, dégagez-vous. Si vous ne pouvez pas venir à pied, venez en carrosse ou en chaize-à-porteurs. Car en un mot la compagnie ne peut pas se passer de vous. L'affaire est d'une assez grande délicatesse pour que vous preveniez le zèle et l'empressement qu'on a de vous voir.

"J'ay l'honneur d'être avec respect, Monsieur et très cher Confrère, votre très humble et très obéissant serviteur.

"De Girardin."[2]

The "affaire d'une grande délicatesse" seems to have been the "project," whatever it was, referred to by Wake in the following reply to Beauvoir, dated February 9th (O.S.), 1719-20. If so, it is evident that Wake did not expect much from it.

"I heartily wish there were either spirit or inclination enough in the Sorbonne to go with our friend the Abbé's project. But the fire decays; men's inclinations cool; the Court will do nothing; and you are very sensible that without the Court nothing can be done in any such affair.

"Nevertheless, their good opinion of the Church of England should be kept up as much as possible. We should encourage them all we can to account of us as of brethren, who have only thrown off, what they are weary of, the tyranny of the Court of Rome, without any change in any fundamental article either of the doctrine or govern-

---

[1] *Wake Corresp.*, cclxii., No. 77.
[2] *Beauvoir Corresp.*, No. 12.

ment of the Catholic Church. And upon this ground I shall be ready to continue a brotherly correspondence with any of their great men, provided it be done with such caution as may not expose my letters to be made prisoners to a Secretary of State; a thing which can never become my character, and may carry an ill aspect, even in our own Court, till the thing be rightly understood."[1]

Beauvoir seems to have dutifully followed out the wishes of his superior, in paving the way to a "brotherly correspondence" with leading men of the French Church.

"We went some days ago," he writes to Wake, February 15th, 1719-20, "to visit Dr Lambert,[2] a very leading man of the Sorbon, who hath a great deal of spirit and vigour, and seem'd pleas'd with my freedom in deploring the hardships so great a part of the Latin Church lyes under, [under] the oppression of the Court of Rome.

"Dr Leger,[3] another very leading member of the Sorbon, happen'd to come in, and receiv'd me very kindly. Both appear inclinable to peace and unity, and the greatest sticklers against the Constitution *Unigenitus*. The latter is pretty well worn out by age. However, his opinion is of very great weight in the Faculty."[4]

On March 23rd, 1720, De Girardin writes to inform the Archbishop of the submission of De Noailles to the Papal Court, which was about to be made by his signing a qualified acceptance of the *Unigenitus*:

"L'on parle encore fort diversement de l'acceptation future de M. le Card. de Noailles. Les jésuites crient *tolle, tolle!* parceque, disent ils, il reçoit, il adopte plutôt son propre Corps de Doctrine que la Constitution."[5]

De Girardin goes on to describe the terms in which the acceptance was to be couched:

"'À ces causes nous recevons avec soumission et avec respect la Constitution de notre Saint Père le Pape Clément XI., qui commence

---

[1] Maclaine, p. 198.

[2] Lambert, according to Le Roy (p. 577), was the one who discovered the way out of the difficulty, at the stormy meeting of the Sorbonne, related above (p. 39), in the formula: *Censeo obtemperandum, non deliberandum.*"

[3] Described as "un des chefs du parti gallican modéré." *Ib.*, p. 579.

[4] *Wake Corresp.*, cclxii., No. 81.

[5] *Ib.*, No. 22.

par ces mots: *Unigenitus Dei Filius*, selon les explications cy-dessus mentionnées, qui en contiennent le *vray* sens;[1] lesquelles explications n'ont été uniquement données, que pour prévenir les abus qu'on en pouroit faire. . . .'"

This was not the only letter on the subject written by Girardin; and Wake acknowledges them in a letter to Beauvoir, April 19th (O.S.), 1720, with which this correspondence may fitly close:

". . . I perceive, by some late letters from him [Dr. Piers] that he begins to despair of the business of the Constitution. He has reason. The Cardinal de Noailles is ensnared, and has gone too far to retire. The new Archbishop of Cambray will be a Cardinal; and this affair of the Constitution must procure the *calot* for him. The Regent himself is afraid of the Spanish party and the Jesuits; and he will gain, or at least appease them.

"For all these reasons, the doctrine of the Church, and the Gallican liberties, must be abandoned; and on the slight pretence of a comm^t,[2] of no esteem with the opposite party, an accommodation will certainly be made, and those who will not voluntarily go shall be driven into it.

"If our poor friend[3] be one of those who must hereby suffer, why may he not consider of a retreat hither? and, since he cannot yet bring on an union with the two Churches, unite himself with ours, from which, I am sure, his principles and, I believe, his inclinations, are not greatly distant? But this must be managed very tenderly, and rather by a kind of rallying than a direct proposal of it. If he inclines to it, he will easily understand your meaning: if not, 'tis best not to go on far with him in a matter in which you will have no good success."[4]

With these words, ominous, or rather descriptive, of failure, the series of letters ends. The want of success in the negotia-

---

[1] "Quel mensonge," interpolates Girardin, after this word.

[2] A commandment (?) "mandement."

[3] The reference appears to be to De Girardin. If so, he afterwards became a guest of the Archbishop, as here suggested. Writing to Father Courayer, December 9th, 1721, Wake speaks of "our good friend the Abbé Girardin, being still here." . . . "While the Abbé has been here," he adds, "he has had the opportunity of seeing the confirmation of one Bishop, and the consecration of two. When he returns, he will give you a full account of what he observed in both."

[4] Maclaine, p. 199.

tions—a success of which Wake, to do him justice, never appears to have been sanguine—was due to a combination of causes; the death of Du Pin, the vacillation of De Noailles, the sudden energy of the self-seeking Dubois. Those who admit no possibility of unity in the Church of Christ except through submission to the see of Rome, will, of course, point with triumph to the result of the whole transaction, as one more instance of the failure of all attempts to shake the immovable Rock of Peter. Whether they are wholly in the right or not, will be the subject of some remarks later on. For the present, we must conclude this chapter with a short examination of the *Commonitorium* of Du Pin.

Considering what a mass of letters and papers has been preserved from the correspondence of Archbishop Wake,[1] it is somewhat remarkable that neither Du Pin's original draft of the *Commonitorium*, which is known to have been sent to him, nor any copy of it, has been discovered. One such copy is probably to be found among the archives of the Vatican, as Du Pin's papers, after being impounded and examined by the French government, were sent to Rome. The loss, if it prove final, is, as Dr. Pusey says, "exceedingly to be regretted." We possess, however, a tolerably full abstract of the document made by Maclaine, and with this we must be content.

[1] These have never yet been thoroughly examined and catalogued, so that it is difficult to say what may not be in them. In 1758 an inventory of them was begun by Edward Bentham, and continued for some years, being completed in 1766 by an Index drawn up by Dr. Ducarel, the Librarian of Lambeth. But the work was superficially done. Bentham expresses the opinion that "had the collection been made by Archbishop Wake himself, instead of by his Librarian, I am persuaded he would have burnt half of the Letters, and would thereby have given a greater dignity to the Collection." Ducarel seems to have done the best he could with Bentham's materials; but the incompleteness of the Index (numbered in the Lambeth Library 1,133) will be obvious, when it is mentioned that the items "Du Pin," "Gallican Church," "Girardin," are not found in it. In 1867 a catalogue of the MSS. in the Library of Christ Church was compiled by the Rev. G. W. Kitchin, M.A. This includes the Wake MSS., but gives only a general description of the contents of each volume. I was at one time in hopes that the *Commonitorium* might have been found in

According, then, to Maclaine, the author of the *Commonitorium*, after beginning with some reflections on the Reformation, and the present state of the Church of England, proceeded to reduce the controversy between the Churches to three heads: (1) *Articles of Faith;* (2) *Rules and Ceremonies of Ecclesiastical Discipline;* (3) *Moral Doctrine,* or, Rules of Practice. With these to guide him, Du Pin entered on an examination of the XXXIX. Articles of the English Church.

The result of that investigation is thus summed up by Dr. Pusey:[1]—He "approved unconditionally of twenty-three of our Articles; passed over that on the Homilies (No. XXXV.) as not knowing them; proposed slight explanations of ten; so that there remained a difficulty in regard to five only: and on these also he mostly offered explanations of the Roman doctrine."

The first class, those to which he took no exception, were I.-V. (Of the Trinity, etc.); VII. (Of the Old Testament); VIII. (Of the three Creeds); IX. (Of Original Sin); XII. (Of good Works); XV. (Of Christ alone without Sin); XVI. (Of Sin after Baptism); XVII. (Of Predestination and Election); XVIII. (Of obtaining Salvation only by the Name of Christ); XXIII. (Of ministering in the Congregation); XXIV. (Of speaking in the Congregation in such a Tongue as the People understandeth); XXVI. (Of the Unworthiness of Ministers); XXVII. (Of Baptism); XXX. (Of Communion in both Kinds); XXXII. (Of the Marriage of Priests); XXXIII. (Of excommunicate Persons); XXXIV. (Of the Traditions of the

---

Archbishop Tenison's Library; since Wake, we are told, sent many papers relating to the English Church to Courayer, and Courayer "gave his books to the Library of St. Martin's Parish in London (Archbishop Tenison's Library)." See the Introduction to the Oxford edition of the *Dissertation*, 1844, p. ix. But Mr. E. M. Borrajo, of the Guildhall Library, has kindly taken the trouble to ascertain for me that Archbishop Tenison's Library was sold, under a scheme of the Charity Commissioners, in 1861; and that the Sale Catalogue, preserved in the British Museum, does not contain any entry likely to have included the desired papers. The MSS. were sold on July 1st, 1861.

[1] *Eirenicon,* 1865, p. 213.

Church); XXXVIII. (Of Christian Men's Goods, which are not common); XXXIX. (Of a Christian Man's Oath).

Dr. Pusey does not specify which he considered to be the ten accepted by Du Pin with qualifications, and which the five objected to by him; but I think we shall be right in grouping them as follows.

The second class, those conditionally admitted, were: VI. (Of the Sufficiency of the Holy Scriptures); X. (Of Free Will); XI. (Of the Justification of Man); XIII. (Of Works before Justification); XIV. (Of Works of Supererogation); XIX. (Of the Church); XX. (Of the Authority of the Church); XXI. (Of the Authority of General Councils); XXXVI. (Of Consecration of Bishops and Ministers); XXXVII. (Of the Civil Magistrates).

The remainder, about which alone any serious difficulty was raised, consisted of: XXII. (Of Purgatory); XXV. (Of the Sacraments); XXVIII. (Of the Lord's Supper); XXIX. (Of the Wicked, which eat not, etc.); XXXI. (Of the one Oblation of Christ finished upon the Cross).

Beginning with the last, and most important class, we will note what the points were to which the Gallican doctor took exception.

With regard to Article XXII., Du Pin is represented[1] as observing (1) "that souls must be purged, that is, purified from all defilement of sin, before they are admitted to celestial bliss; (2) that the Church of Rome doth not affirm this to be done by fire; (3) that indulgences are only relaxations or remissions of temporal penalties in this life; (4) that the Roman Catholics do not worship the cross, or relics, or images, or even saints before their images, but only pay them an external respect, which is not of a religious nature; and that even this external demonstration of respect is a matter of indifference, which may be laid aside or retained without harm."

---

[1] It must be remembered that we have only Maclaine's version to depend upon, as he rarely gives the original Latin.

In spite of Maclaine's comment upon this, that "the Doctor endeavours to mince matters as nicely as he can, to see if he can make the cable[1] pass through the eye of the needle," as though to imply that here agreement was hopeless, I cannot see that in the first of these propositions any insuperable barrier is raised. At present, indeed, we stand as on the widely-separated banks of a broad river: but if we could re-ascend the stream, past the writings of Bellarmine, past the decrees of the Council of Trent, up to the Platonic theories of Origen, we might find little to divide us. As to (2) Du Pin admits that the purgatorial cleansing is not to be by fire—meaning, I suppose, material fire. If so, he differs in this from Bellarmine. In affirming (3) that "indulgences are only relaxations or remissions of temporal penalties *in this life*," he contradicts the modern doctrine of the Church of Rome, which retains, indeed, the word *temporal* in this connection, but includes under the term the pains of purgatory.[2] With regard to (4) it is obvious that if such was the language of Du Pin, there is nothing to keep him aloof from us.

In his comments on Article XXV., Du Pin "insists that the five Romish sacraments be acknowledged as such, whether instituted immediately by Christ, or not." To this the reply would be, that all turns on the right definition of terms. Two of these seven mysteries were "ordained by Christ Himself." These, therefore, we distinguish from the rest, just as Cardinal Bessarion did in 1436.[3] There can be no objection to the word *sacrament* being used to designate each of the remaining five, so long as it is understood to be used, for the reason just stated, in a lower and secondary sense.

As regards the crucial Article XXVIII., and its corollary XXIX., our account of what Du Pin wished to have altered is too brief to be satisfactory:—" He proposes expressing that

[1] The unauthorized various reading for *camel* in Matt. xix. 24.
[2] Browne: *Exposition of the Thirty-nine Articles*, ed. 1894, p. 503.
[3] Pusey: *Eirenicon*, p. 218. Dr. Pusey breaks off into a long discussion of the "Anointing of the Sick," in its practical working; but this does not affect the main argument.

part of the XXVIIIth that relates to *Transubstantiation* (which term he is willing to omit entirely), in the following manner: 'That the bread and wine are really changed into the body and blood of Christ; which last are truly and really received by all, though none but the faithful partake of any benefit from them.' This extends also to the XXIXth Article."

As to the first part of this statement, it would seem that all turns on the meaning of the word "changed." Such a "change" may cover what Romanists mean by Transubstantiation.[1] Otherwise, in what follows as to the reception, there is nothing diverse from the language of our Catechism, except in the last clause. We say that "the Body and Blood of Christ are verily and indeed taken and received *by the faithful* in the Lord's Supper." Du Pin, agreeing in this with the majority of believers in Transubstantiation,[2] held that *all* did "truly and really" receive, though not to their benefit. On the whole, as long as the ambiguous "changed into" remains, we cannot say that we are brought much nearer to agreement by this statement of Du Pin; except, indeed, that the debateable ground is narrowed by the very conciseness of the statement.

"On the XXXIst Article," according to Maclaine, Du Pin "is less inclined to concessions; and maintains that the sacrifice of Christ is not only *commemorated*, but *continued*, in the Eucharist, and that every communicant offers Him along with the priest."

In this case also the difference may at the bottom be one of words and names. Dr. Pusey[3] quotes from Bishop Cosins a sentence almost identical with this of Du Pin: "We still *continue and commemorate* that Sacrifice, which Christ once made upon the Cross." "In a certain sense," wrote the late Bishop of Winchester, "we may be said to offer His all-pre-

---

[1] Dr. Pusey sums up his remarks on this subject in the words: "My own conviction is, that our Articles deny Transubstantiation in one sense, and that the Roman Church, according to the explanation of the Catechism of the Council of Trent, affirms it in another."—*Eirenicon*, p. 229.

[2] Browne: as before, p. 726.

[3] *Eirenicon*, p. 230.

vailing sacrifice before the mercy-seat of God, when, with the consecrated symbols of His Body and Blood before us, we approach the Table of the Lord, to be fed by Him with the food of everlasting life."[1] "*We* may be said to offer," says the Church of England expositor. "Every communicant offers Him," says the French theologian. Both alike shut out the idea of a sacrificing *Hiereus*, and suggest rather the presenting to the Father, the pleading before Him, on the part of the worshippers, of the one all-sufficient oblation and satisfaction for the sins of the whole world.

If such be the *difficulties* raised by Du Pin, we shall not expect to find anything very formidable in the *qualifications* with which he would accept the ten Articles assigned to the second class.

The first of these is Article VI., which affirms the sufficiency of the Holy Scriptures for Salvation. On this he remarks: "This we will readily admit,[2] provided that Tradition be not excluded, which does not exhibit new articles of faith, but confirms and explains what is contained in the Sacred Writings, and fortifies it with new safeguards against those who are otherwise minded; so that there is no statement of new things, but of old things in a new way."

None would wish to exclude Tradition, so long as the claim made on its behalf is not one for equal and concurrent authority, but only for the subservient office of a handmaid. "It is not true," says the writer we have before quoted,[3] "that the Church of England rejects the proper use of tradition, though she will not suffer it to be unduly exalted. She does not reject the testimony of antiquity, and cut herself off from the Communion of the Saints of old."

---

[1] *On the Articles*, as before, p. 743.
[2] Here we have the Latin to fall back upon: "Hoc lubenter admittemus, modo non excludatur Traditio, quæ articulos Fidei novos non exhibet, sed confirmat et explicat ea quæ in Sacris Literis habentur, ac adversus aliter sapientes munit eos novis cautionibus; ita ut non nova dicantur, sed antiqua nove."
[3] *On the Articles*, p. 175.

As regards the list of apocryphal books appended to this Article, Du Pin is of opinion that they will not occasion much difficulty. He is inclined to decide that "they ought to be deemed canonical, as those books concerning which there were doubts for some time:"[1] yet, since they are not in the first, or Jewish, canon, "he will allow them to be called *Deutero-canonical.*"

The reservation attached to Article X. is a purely scholastic one. "He consents to the Xth Article, which relates to Freewill, provided that by the word *power* be understood what School divines call *potentia proxima*, or a direct and immediate power;[2] since, without a *remote* power of doing good works, sin could not be imputed."

The wording of the next comment, on Article XI., is not clear in the Latin.[3] Maclaine translates, but not very exactly: "We do not deny that it is by faith alone that we are justified; but we maintain that faith, charity, and good works, are necessary to salvation: and this is acknowledged in the following (XIIth) Article."

The only reserve Du Pin has in approving Article XIII., is that he thinks it "somewhat harsh to affirm that all the actions which are not done in pursuance of the grace of Christ, are sins."[4] At the same time he would not have discussions on the subject, except among divines. Our Article, in point of fact, does not declare such acts to "be sins," but to "have the nature of sin."

On Article XIV., which treats of Works of Supererogation ("undoubtedly," according to Maclaine, "one of the most

---

[1] The sentence as it stands is hardly logical. Unfortunately, the Latin is not preserved.

[2] "Which plainly it does," is Dr. Pusey's comment on this.

[3] "Fide sola in Christum nos justificari, quod Articulo XI^{mo} exponitur, non inficiamur; sed fide, charitate, et adjunctis bonis operibus, quæ omnino necessaria sunt ad salutem, ut articulo sequenti agnoscitur."

[4] "De articulo XIII^{mo} nulla lis erit, cum multi theologi in eadem versentur sententia. Durius videtur id dici, eas omnes actiones, quæ ex gratia Christi non fiunt, esse peccata. Nolim tamen de hac redisceptari, nisi inter theologos."

absurd and pernicious doctrines of the Romish Church"), Du Pin remarks that "Works of *Supererogation* mean only works conducive to salvation, which are not matters of strict *precept*, but of *counsel* only: that the word, being new,[1] may be rejected, provided it be owned that the faithful do some such good works."

In the definition of "The Church," in Article XIX., he would have inserted the words "under lawful pastors" (after the words "a congregation of faithful men"?). It was also his opinion that, "though all particular Churches, even that of Rome, may err, it is needless to say this in a Confession of Faith."

He agrees, with Article XX., that the Church *may* not (*non licet*) "ordain anything that is contrary to God's Word written;" but adds that "it must be taken for granted that the Church will never do this in matters *quæ fidei substantiam evertant*."

"It is in consequence of this notion," says Maclaine, "that he remarks on the XXIst Article, that General Councils, *received by the Universal Church*, cannot err; and that, though particular Councils may, yet every private man has not a right to reject what he thinks contrary to Scripture." The caveat is an important one. It amounts to affirming, as Dr. Pusey points out,[2] that "No General Council, received by the Universal Church, has erred." It is a statement of a fact in the past, not of a present or future possibility. The latter part of Du Pin's sentence only affirms in other words our own statement, as against the uncontrolled liberty of private judgment, that "the Church has authority in matters of faith."

Article XXXVI. is one on which we should have been glad to possess Du Pin's words more exactly. According

---

[1] I have not been able to trace the first appearance of the word *supererogatio*, as an ecclesiastical term. Tyndale uses it (*Doctrinal Treatises*, Park. Soc., p. 86). The verb *supererogare* is found in the Vulgate of St. Luke, x. 35, as a rendering of the Greek word for "to spend more," "to pay over and above."

[2] *Eirenicon*, p. 216.

to Maclaine, "he would not have the English ordinations pronounced null, though some of them, perhaps, are so; but thinks that, if an union be made, the English clergy ought to be continued in their offices and benefices, either by right or indulgence: *sive ex jure, sive ex indulgentia ecclesiæ*."

The language used, so far as we can judge of it in this condensed form, seems at first to imply doubt, coupled with a willingness to give us the benefit of the doubt. But on closer examination it implies more than this. If the English clergy were to remain in their benefices, in the event of a reunion, we must assume that Du Pin was satisfied with the validity of their ordination. No "indulgence of the Church" could make valid that which was *ab initio* invalid.[1]

But we have other evidence on this point. Before le Père Courayer published, in 1723, the first edition of his well-known *Dissertation*, he had been in frequent correspondence with Archbishop Wake, who put into his hands various "original papers" and letters which had passed between him and the theologians on the Continent.[2] The author of the article "Wake" in the old edition of the *Biographia Britannica* had before him, when he wrote, no fewer than forty-five letters from the Archbishop to Courayer, bearing date 1721 to 1727.[3] Though the probability is only slight, it is more likely that the "original papers" furnished by Wake to Courayer would contain favourable opinions on the validity of English Orders, than the reverse. And, among these papers, none were more likely to be included than what had been written by Du Pin.

There is no need, however, to be content with mere presumptions. Du Pin and De Girardin, as Beauvoir writes,[4] a few months after the date of the *Commonitorium*, are "extremely satisfied with the account of the succession of the

---

[1] The argument is Dr. Pusey's.—*Eirenicon*, p. 231.
[2] Bowyer's *Anecdotes*, 1782, p. 84.
[3] Courayer: *Dissertation on the Validity, &c.*, 1844, Introd. p. xvii *n*. See also the note above, p. 107.
[4] See above, p. 73.

English bishops. For before they were in error about it." And Du Pin himself wrote to Wake:[1]

"I was exceedingly pleased with what you were so good as to write to me so elegantly and accurately about the election and consecration of the Bishops in England. It does not seem to me to differ much from the customs which flourished in the time of Charlemagne, as is clear from the Capitulars of this and the following Emperors, and the formulæ of Marculfus. And I cannot sufficiently praise the precautions which you use to prevent any unworthy person from stealing into the Episcopate. Would that Bishops were proved in the same way everywhere, before they were consecrated!"[2]

Lastly, as to Article XXXVII., Du Pin "admits it, so far as relates to the authority of the civil power; denies all temporal and all immediate spiritual jurisdiction of the Pope; but alleges that, by virtue of his primacy, which moderate Church of England men do not deny, he is bound to see that the true faith be maintained, that the Canons be observed everywhere; and, when anything is done in violation of either, to provide the remedies prescribed for such disorders by the Canon Laws (*secundum leges canonicas, ut malum resarciatur procurare*). As to the rest, he is of opinion that every Church ought to enjoy its own liberties and privileges, which the Pope has no right to infringe. He declares against going *too far* in the punishment of heretics, against admitting the Inquisition into France, and against war without a just cause."[3]

To some of Du Pin's proposals in the *Commonitorium* Wake

[1] I give the translation from the *Eirenicon*, p. 232. The original is in the *Wake Corresp.*, cclviii., No. 98.

[2] I have given more space than is perhaps needful to this subject, owing to the interest of late raised in it afresh. A writer in a Roman Catholic monthly periodical, called *S. Luke's* has recently drawn attention to two documents found by Father Gasquet among the archives of the Vatican; one being a copy of a Bull issued by Paul IV., June 12th, 1555, and the other a copy of a Brief, October 30th of the same year; in both of which the orders of those ordained in England by the Edwardine ordinal are declared invalid. See the No. for August, 1895, pp. 122-125. Except to believers in Papal infallibility, this will not appear decisive of the question.

[3] Maclaine, p. 155.

declared, almost with warmth, that he would never submit.[1] Possibly one of these was that with which we are now concerned. To admit that it was the Pope's duty, or prerogative, to see that the canon laws be observed *everywhere*, and to provide the remedies prescribed by the same laws, might have seemed an infringement of the rights of each bishop in his own diocese. If so, any misunderstanding was cleared up by a further interchange of opinion. On December 1st, 1718, Du Pin wrote to Wake:[2]

"In regard to the jurisdiction of the Roman Pontiff, as regards the State, it is restricted within narrow bounds, so that it can be of no prejudice to us. For as to temporals he has no power; and in spirituals he is held within the rules of the ancient Canons. He can do nothing in those things which relate to the government of the Bishop in his own Diocese; he cannot ordain or enact anything pertaining to discipline; he cannot excommunicate anyone, or claim anything else to himself.

"His primacy (namely, that he holds the first place among Bishops, as all antiquity affirms, and the Greeks themselves, although rent from the Roman Church, confess) we acknowledge. But that Primacy does not give him a higher grade among Bishops: he is only their fellow-bishop, though first among Bishops."

Wake's reply shows how much they were at one on this subject:[3]

"The honour which you give to the Roman Pontiff differs so little, I deem, from that which our sounder Theologians readily grant him, that, on this point, I think, it will not be difficult, on either side, either to agree altogether in the same opinion, or mutually to bear with a dissent of no moment."

We have now seen, so far as the means at our disposal allowed, what was the deliberate judgment of one of the most learned men of the Gallican Church in those days on the doctrines of the Church of England. Even in our Articles,

---

[1] See above, p. 58.
[2] *Wake Corresp.*, cclviii., No. 98. The translation is Dr. Pusey's.
[3] *Ib.*, No. 100; *Eirenicon*, p. 234.

to which the Puritan feels himself nearer than he does to our Liturgy, there has been shown to be but little to which Du Pin took serious exception. More than that, his calm, undogmatizing temper, and his true catholicity of spirit, enabled him to allow for what might be good in what was unfamiliar to him, and to distinguish between trifles and essentials. Wake met him in the same liberal spirit. While "a staunch assertor of the orthodoxy of the Anglican formularies," while "insisting that any doctrinal reforms necessary to reunion must come from the side of Rome," he was anxious "to remove from the Service-books whatever might be a hindrance to intercommunion in religious offices; 'that so, whenever any one comes from us to them, or from them to us, we may all join together in prayers and the holy sacraments.'"[1]

It is difficult to refrain from the belief, that had the matter rested with Du Pin and Archbishop Wake alone, the differences left to separate the Gallican and Anglican Churches would have all but disappeared. The union they both sought after was denied them, at least in outward form, on this side the grave. But their work has not been lost. It has shown, more convincingly than ever, that, in Du Pin's own words, "the controversy between us may easily be settled, if only the fairer Theologians are heard on both sides, if dictating is avoided, and we are led, not by party spirit, but by love of seeking the truth."

[1] Jervis, ii. 441.

CHAPTER IV.

The French Church in Modern Times.

AT the eve of the Revolution, the French Church was in a state of outward grandeur, but with fatal signs of inward decay. According to an authority [1] which we have no desire to call in question, a fifth part of the soil of France was in its possession, with an income arising from this and other sources of upwards of £9,000,000 sterling. The number of those supported by these revenues was equally imposing. The latest researches show an array of 27,000 monks and 37,000 nuns; while 70,000 bishops, priests, and beneficed abbés formed the secular clergy.

But the state of the religious houses in many parts, as at the eve of the Reformation in the sixteenth century, gave a sure presage of the changes impending. Monasteries dying out for want of inmates, a general lukewarmness among the professed, laxity in many institutions, scandals in some:—such are the summaries under which M. Taine groups together the facts he cites.[2] The personal character of the clergy, as a body, is declared, at least by some writers, to have been at this period good. De Tocqueville doubts "if there was ever a body of clergy in the world more remarkable [for their virtues and religious faith] than the Catholic clergy of France at the moment when they were surprised by the Revolution."[3] Yet for all this they were intolerant and blinded with the pride of power. "In 1780 the Assembly of the Clergy declares that 'the

[1] See a paper by the Abbé Martin in the *Nineteenth Century*, December, 1879, pp. 1093-1117, on "The Present State of the French Church."

[2] *Les Origines de la France Contemporaine*, par H. Taine. *La Révolution*, tom. i., 1878, p. 212.

[3] See an article in the *Saturday Review*, July 8th, 1882, p. 58.

altar and the throne would equally be in danger, if heresy were allowed to throw off its shackles.' Even in 1789, the clergy, in its memorials, while consenting to the toleration of non-Catholics, finds the edict of 1788 [1787?] too liberal. They desire that they should be excluded from judicial offices, that they should never be allowed to worship in public, and that mixed marriages should be interdicted."[1] The immunities and privileges enjoyed by an order which was thus intolerant of others helped to swell the accusations against them. It was an act in which some saw a retributive justice that the first blow struck at them came from one of themselves, Talleyrand, Bishop of Autun.

Charles Maurice de Talleyrand-Périgord was a man of keen insight into the course which affairs about him were taking, and of no high principles that would restrain him from turning them to his own account. An unbeliever and a libertine, he played a part not unlike that of Thomas Cromwell, Earl of Essex, with the added reproach of being himself not a layman but a cleric. He it was who, in a speech in the National Assembly, on October 10th, 1789, advocated the right of the State to confiscate the property of such religious houses as it thought desirable to suppress, and in other ways to appropriate the revenues of the Church. "It was a strange phenomenon," says Jervis,[2] "a prelate of the Church, a man born in the highest ranks of the aristocracy, the possessor of rich preferment and enviable worldly position, standing up in the Legislature to propose a measure for disinheriting his own order, destroying their independence, and degrading them to the level of mere hirelings of the State."

Within the short compass of an essay it is impossible to do more than indicate very briefly the course of these events. It was, as has been said, a reaping of the dragon's teeth sown by Louis XIV. The harsh measures adopted in his reign against

[1] Taine: *The Ancient Régime*, tr. by Durand, 1876, p. 63. For the edict of November, 1787, see Félice: *Histoire des Protestants de France*, 1880, p. 576.
[2] *Gallican Church*, 1882, p. 30.

the Jansenists now brought their retribution. Martineau, a Jansenist, followed up the proposals of the Bishop of Autun by bringing forward a measure for the suppression of sinecure benefices, and for the extinction of religious houses with fewer than twenty inmates—a measure that only led the way to far more sweeping confiscations. Camus, another member of the same party, had a chief hand in formulating the *Constitution civile du Clergé*. By this notorious enactment, drawn up by the Ecclesiastical Committee of the Assembly, in pursuance of an order of February 6th, 1790,[1] it was decreed, among a number of articles, that every Department should form a single diocese, coextensive with the Department (Article I.), that, "without prejudice to the unity of the faith and of the communion maintained with the visible head of the Universal Church," no French church, or parish, or individual citizen, should acknowledge the authority of any ordinary or metropolitan seated within the territories of a foreign power (Article V.); that stipends, at a fixed rate, should be paid to the clergy, according to their degree, making them thus salaried officers of the State (Titre III., Articles iii.-vi.). These and other provisions, by which the Church of France was delivered up, bound hand and foot, to the civil government, produced, as might be expected, the most violent disorders. Fifty bishoprics were suppressed at a blow. Cathedral and collegiate chapters were dissolved. The old boundaries of dioceses and parishes were disturbed, and old associations wantonly shocked. The covenanted stipends, it is needless to say, were not long paid.

Harder to bear than the loss of livelihood was the imposition of an oath upon the clergy of France that they would maintain the *Constitution civile* to the utmost of their power. This was in the beginning of December, 1790. The effect of the oath was at once to divide the clergy into two hostile parties, the jurors and non-jurors, the minority who accepted, and the great majority who refused it. In case of a number of the bishops the acceptance implied their acquiescence in the suppression of their sees. If they, or any of the inferior clergy,

[1] Guettée, xii. 221, where the full text is given.

THE FRENCH CHURCH IN MODERN TIMES. 121

refused, the punishment was to be forfeiture of stipends, deprivation of civil rights, incapacity for any public office, with heavier penalties still looming in the background.[1] The numbers of those who submitted, and of those who set the Assembly at defiance and braved the consequences, are variously given. The Abbé Martin declares [2] that out of a hundred and forty-eight bishops, to whom the oath was tendered in 1791, a hundred and forty-one refused, and only seven accepted. There is no need to enter into details of the sufferings and persecutions endured by the French clergy for the next ten years; the scenes of violence and bloodshed in churches; the sentencing to the galleys, to execution; the flight to other countries, which brought many a poor curé as an emigrant to our own shores. However bitter the cup which the French Church, in the days of its power, had made the despised nonconformists drink of, there was no denying that the retribution brought upon itself was bravely borne. The beginning of the present century beheld it in one sense humbled to the dust, but in another emerging purified and chastened from the fire of persecution, and endeared to the people by the very spectacle of its suffering.

Our chief object in referring to this dark picture is to show by what ties the Church of France became drawn more closely to the Papal See, and gradually lost something of its old national character. It was in the Pope that it found a friend, in the hour of its utmost need, who could give it help, and, when that failed, could at least give it sympathy. On March 10th, 1791, Pius VI. issued a brief, condemning the principles of the Revolution in general, and the obnoxious articles of the *Constitution civile* in particular.[3] This was followed up by

---

[1] Jervis, iii. 96.   [2] Article before quoted, p. 1093.
[3] Jervis, iii., pp. 137-139. The Abbé Guettée (xii., p. 218) thinks that Pius VI. might have guided the acts of the Assembly, in their earlier stages, had he possessed the requisite knowledge, instead of thwarting and thereby making them more bitterly hostile. He regards the Ecclesiastical Commission as composed of men "sincèrement dévoués à l'Église; mais, per malheur, on lui fit voir dès ennemis en ceux qu'il eût dû considérer comme des enfants."

another, dated April 13th of the same year, in which the chief agents of the attack upon the Church were excommunicated, and suspension from their spiritual functions was pronounced against all ecclesiastics who had submitted to the state Constitution, unless within forty days they retracted their oath of allegiance to it. Whether the Pope was wise and far-sighted in this, or not, it is certain that many retractations followed; that the non-jurors felt themselves strengthened and encouraged in their resistance; and that the eyes of the French clergy in general became more turned to Rome, as the quarter from whence they might look for spiritual support.

Pius VI. died in exile at Valence in Dauphiné, August 29th, 1799, in his eighty-second year, but his successor, Pius VII. kept up the same line of policy. But with the new century the prospect of affairs began to lighten. Bonaparte was now First Consul, and his sagacious eye perceived the accession of strength that would come to him, if he could have the clergy on his side, or at least disarm their hostility. Hence the negotiations begun with the Pope, negotiations broken off and resumed again and again, but which finally resulted in the Concordat, settled on July 15th, 1801, and of which the ratifications were exchanged on September 18th [1] following.

The most important of the seventeen articles included in the Concordat was the first:—"La religion catholique, apostolique et romaine sera librement exercée en France. Son culte sera public, en se conformant aux règlements de police que le gouvernement jugera nécessaires pour la tranquillité publique." The wording of the last clause had been fiercely contested; but on the whole, if we consider through what a chaos of disordered opinions and infidel excesses the country had passed during the ten years preceding, it will seem an immense advance towards the restoration of the peace of the Church, that the free exercise of the Catholic religion should be per-

---

[1] So the Abbé Martin. Guettée (xii. 413) says Sepember 10th. The text of the "Convention" is given in full by Guettée. I have not had an opportunity of seeing the work of Georges Raux, published this year: *La République et le Concordat de* 1801.

mitted in France, even under these restrictions. Nominations to vacant bishoprics were to be made by the First Consul, but canonical institution thereto was to be given by the Pope (Article V.). Before entering on their office, all bishops were to take a prescribed oath of obedience and fidelity to the government established by the constitution of the State (Article VI.). The bishops were to nominate to parochial cures, but their choice was limited to persons accepted by the government (Article X.). The Pope, on his part, agreed not to disturb the possessors of alienated ecclesiastical property (Article XIII.). The government was to provide a suitable stipend for the bishops and the parochial clergy (Article XIV.). The Holy See recognized, in the person of the First Consul of the French Republic, the possessor of the same rights and privileges as had been held by the old government (Article XVI.).

It is clear that by this last stipulation what had been known as Gallicanism was formally recognized, if not re-established, in France. But, as though that were not enough, the government endeavoured to strengthen its own hands still more by appending to the Concordat a string of no fewer than seventy-seven "Articles Organiques," the heading of the first eight of which, *Du régime de l'Église catholique dans ses rapports avec les droits et la police de l'État*, sufficiently indicates their general purpose.[1] The excuse, or justification, for adding these Articles, was found in the language of the first and sixteenth Articles of the Concordat, which provided that the restored public worship should conform to the police regulations of the government; and that the First Consul, as representing the State, should enjoy the rights and privileges in ecclesiastical matters enjoyed by the government before the Revolution. It was easy to expand these provisos into a fresh code of regulations. In this way powers were claimed for the civil government, exceeding anything that Louis XIV. would have insisted on. No Bull, or other instrument, emanating from the Court of Rome, was to be published, printed, or put into execution in France, without the sanction of the government (Article I.).

[1] They are given in full by Guettée, xii. 416-422.

All cases of *abuse* on the part of the superior clergy were to be referred to the Council of State (Article VI.); and these *cas d'abus* were made to include a number of acts which the clergy might have supposed to be within their own proper jurisdiction. Even the nomination and institution by bishops of persons to hold parochial cures were to be first approved by the head of the State, before they could take effect (Article XIX.). No church *fête* might be instituted, without leave of the government (Article XLI.). In towns where there were churches of other denominations than the Catholic, no out-door ceremonies (including, of course, processions) were to be permitted to the Catholics (Article XLV.). The very dress of the clergy was prescribed. Public prayers might be directed by government; in which case the bishops must confer with the prefects and commandants of the district. In a word, the most jealous care was taken that there should be no infringement of "the rights, franchises and customs of the Gallican Church" (Article VI.); but no anxiety was shown to avoid trenching on what the Pope had been used to regard as his rights.

The Concordat, with these Organic Articles appended to it, was brought before the Assembly on April 5th, 1802, recommended to their acceptance in a brilliant speech of the Minister of Public Worship, Portalis; and two days later was passed with acclaim by both houses of the legislature.[1] On Easter Monday, April 19th, a solemn service was held in Notre Dame, to commemorate the restoration of peace in Europe, and the reconciliation of France with the Catholic Church.

In Rome, as might be expected, the news of this equivocal proceeding of the French government was received with irritation and alarm. Pius VII. had made repeated concessions, for the sake of peace, that the Concordat pure and simple might be agreed upon. Now, to his unspeakable vexation, he found that he had been outwitted, and that what had just been enrolled as part of the statute-law of France, was not the mere text he had assented to, but the text glossed

[1] Jervis, iii. 384.

with the commentary of the opposing party. His indignation showed itself in an allocution in Consistory, delivered on May 20th following;[1] but his remonstrances produced little effect, and Bonaparte went on unchecked in his course.

We must pass rapidly over the events preceding the fall of Napoleon, which may be said to have begun with the occupation of Rome by the French troops in the early part of 1808. The Pope was kept a prisoner at Savona, a small town in Northern Italy, under the government of France. There he resorted for defence to one of the few weapons left him, the same which had been used by Innocent XI. in his dispute with Louis XIV. He was entitled, by the fifth Article of the Concordat, without taking count of what he would have held to be his right, to confer canonical institution on all Bishops of the French Church, after their nomination by the government. No provision had been made as to the length of time which might expire before this was done, or as to the course to be pursued if the Pope refused such institution altogether. Accordingly, an increasing number of newly-appointed French bishops found themselves in the painful dilemma of either siding with the civil power, and entering on their episcopal office without receiving the Papal sanction, or of showing canonical obedience to the Pope, at the risk of offending the civil government. Cardinal Maury, in accepting the Emperor's nomination to the Archbishopric of Paris, was an example of one line of conduct; Cardinal Fesch, Napoleon's own uncle, who had previously refused that elevation, was an example of the other. The schism among the clergy thus produced threatened to become dangerous; and still more so when Napoleon, under pretence of removing the Pope from a spot whence the English fleet might have carried him off to Sicily or Malta, had him hastily conveyed, at the risk of his life, to Fontainebleau. There he extorted from him the Concordat

---

[1] Jervis, iii. 388. The Abbé Martin, in the article before quoted, p. 1096, says that, if the Organic Articles were now put in force, "it would become the inauguration of the most violent persecutions to which the Catholic Church has ever been subjected." He cites in evidence Articles I., III., XI.

of Fontainebleau, January 25th, 1813. By virtue of this, provision was made for the institution by the metropolitan of any bishop, nominated by the government, whom the Pope refused, or delayed for more than six months, to institute.[1] Pius VII. bitterly repented the concessions he had made, almost as soon as they had been wrung from him, and showed his grief in an agony of self-reproach. But it is a singular testimony alike to his forgiving temper, and to the power of fascination exercised by Napoleon on all with whom he came into personal contact, that the aged pontiff treasured up no feeling of resentment against his captor. When the fallen Emperor was pining on the rock of St. Helena, Pius, who had given shelter to several members of his family at Rome, wrote in touching terms to Cardinal Consalvi concerning the exile :—" The pious and courageous initiative of 1801," he said, " has caused us long ago to forget and forgive subsequent injuries. Savona and Fontainebleau are merely faults of the understanding, aberrations of human ambition ; the Concordat was an act of Christian and truly heroic restoration."[2]

After the Bourbons had been reinstated, a Convention was settled between the plenipotentiaries of the French government and of the Pope, by which the Concordat of 1801 was to be set aside, and that of 1516, between Francis I. and Leo X., taken as the basis of agreement. The property of the clergy before the Revolution, so far as it was capable of recovery, was to revert to its former uses. The Organic Articles were to be repealed, " in so far as they were contrary to the laws of the Church."[3] Here, however, an unexpected difficulty arose. The Pope had duly signed the new Concordat. But when it was presented to the French legislature, so many objections were taken, that the scheme had to be finally abandoned. For a time the clergy in France were left in a state of unsettlement between the two Concordats, one of which had been repudiated by the Pope, and the other rejected by the legislature. Matters

[1] Jervis, iii. 487.
[2] *Ib.*, p. 495, quoting the *Mémoires du Cardinal Consalvi*, Introd. p. 78.
[3] *Ib.*, p. 498.

were partially adjusted by a Bull of October 10th, 1822, in virtue of which thirty new dioceses were created, raising the total number to eighty. The Bull itself was accepted in France with a saving clause, exempting from approval anything in it which might be "contrary to the constitutional Charter, to the laws of the kingdom, or to the franchises, liberties, or maxims of the Gallican Church."[1]

The great mistake made at the Bourbon restoration was the same, though in another form, as that which had been made by Napoleon himself. In both cases it was clearly shown that the great object of the civil power was to use the Church as a buttress for itself. Napoleon would have made the papacy a French patriarchate, with the Pope at Paris. Louis XVIII., in his charter of 1814, proclaimed the freedom of public worship, and the toleration of all forms of religious belief. But he declared the Catholic religion to be that of the State, and his conduct throughout his reign showed that he regarded it as, more than all else, a counterpoise to the principles of the Revolution. Its spirit must now be essentially conservative, reactionary. This line of policy, it need hardly be said, was sure to weaken the ties of restored affection in which the Church had begun to be held by the nation at large. Louis had offended the veterans of the Consulate by affecting to *grant* a charter, as of his own gracious condescension, instead of admitting that he came to the throne by virtue of it.[2] His adherents increased this ill-feeling by widening the breach between the Revolution and the religion of the State. The clergy, to their own loss, were but too ready to follow this lead. It was natural that men who had suffered, or whose immediate predecessors had suffered, so much in those political convulsions, should look back upon them with dislike. And so they became reactionary. They viewed with favour the re-establishment by Pius VII. of the order of the Jesuits, in 1814, which had been suppressed by Clement XIV. in 1773. They became active in interdicting public amusements on

[1] Jervis, iii. 499.
[2] Bonnechose: *Hist. de France* (tr. by Robson), p. 648.

Sundays and Holy-days, talked of recovering their tithes and domains, and inveighed against the owners of their former possessions.[1] This was hardly to be wondered at, but it tended to make the Church of the Restoration unpopular. The obstinacy of Charles X., and his blind insensibility to the wishes of the nation, intensified this feeling, till, as persons still living can remember, "in 1830, a Catholic priest could scarcely show himself in the street."[2]

From the danger thus threatening it, the Church was saved by the efforts of a knot of ardent politicians, ultramontane at heart, but advocating the cause of civil and religious liberty. These men—Lacordaire, Lamennais, Montalembert, and others—strove to show that the Catholic religion was compatible with republican principles as well as monarchical, in fact, with political liberty of every kind. In this they carried their doctrines too far, and had to be called to order by an encyclical of Gregory XVI., August 15th, 1832.[3] The revolutionary proceedings of February, 1848, so far seconded the efforts of these writers that the wealthier classes, afraid of the spread of socialism, if not of another Reign of Terror, were driven back to conservatism, and to a closer alliance with the Church.[4] How serious had been the danger, during the years preceding that outbreak, of the French Church becoming the Church of the rich and well-to-do alone, is strikingly shown by the *Diary in France*, 1845, of Dr. Christopher Wordsworth. At the fashionable churches, says that writer, "all the well-known evils of our own pew-system are repeated over again with chairs, with even a little extra disorder and confusion, to be

---

[1] Bonnechose, p. 649.

[2] M. Prevost-Paradol: *France* (two Lectures delivered in Edinburgh 1869), p. 49. The writer adds that "the time of the bitterest opposition of our middle classes against the Catholic Church is the time of the Restoration—that is, when the royal government was seen in close alliance with the Church, and when both seemed about to wage a common and deadly war against the most legitimate interests issuing from and connected with the Revolution."

[3] Jervis, iii., 501.

[4] Prevost-Paradol, as before, p. 50.

ascribed to the payment at the time, and to the continual passing and repassing of the person who collects it."[1] For the luxurious, the front rows of chairs have velvet paddings. This picture had its almost inevitable counterpart. In the country, the small peasant-proprietor would not go to church himself, but would "wait for his wife outside, talking and marketing with his neighbours."[2] Yet M. Prevost-Paradol, whose words these last-quoted are, writing some five-and-twenty years after Dr. Wordsworth, bears witness that, in France, "the power of the Catholic Church has been on the increase for thirty years or so, and the clerical influence has wonderfully progressed, during that same period, among that same French *bourgeoisie*, upper and lower, which had formerly thrown off so decidedly its allegiance to the Catholic Church."

Passing onwards over another interval of nearly a quarter of a century, we find the Abbé de Broglie confirming the fact of this growing influence, and speaking of it, as is natural, with much more enthusiasm. The bishops have now, he says (in 1892), an authority over their clergy, and exercise a control in their dioceses, much greater than they had before the Revolution.[3] The growth and development of religious orders, which were in many instances dying out before the end of the previous century, have been spontaneous and rapid. In 1871, out of the 750 members composing the National Assembly, 600 were men avowedly religious.[4] When we compare the composition of this with that of some previous Chambers, we are forced, as the Abbé de Broglie justly says, to admit the fact of a great increase of faith in the country, and of attention to the discharge of religious duties. At the same time, this writer, equally with M. Prevost-Paradol, admits the estrangement from the Church of "la grosse masse rurale," to use M. Taine's expression, "qui s'écarte de la foi," and the avowed hostility to it of great bodies of the artisans, hardly relieved by

---

[1] See the *Christian Remembrancer*, vol. x. (1845), p. 361.
[2] Prevost-Paradol, p. 35.
[3] *Le Présent et l'Avenir du Catholicisme en France*, 1892, p. 17.
[4] *Ib.*, p. 236.

the formation of a nucleus of better material—"un noyau, peu nombreux encore, mais solide, d'ouvriers chrétiens."[1]

If we seek for the causes of this great, though, as we see, not unchequered expansion of the Church in France in modern times, we are met, at every step, with evidence of the increasing activity of the ultramontane body,—in other words, of their leaders, the Jesuits.[2] Through the Empress Eugénie, they exercised an unbounded influence over the counsels of the Second Empire. The more moderate principles of the old Gallicanism were fast being forgotten, or were put contemptuously aside. Here and there a stray voice was raised to plead for them, but to no purpose. "Napoleon I.," urged one petitioner to the Emperor in 1861, "re-enacted the four Articles of the French clergy among the laws of the state. May your Majesty continue and complete his work! That will be one of your best titles to renown."[3] The answer to all such petitions was heard in the roar of the guns of Civita Vecchia.

It has been pointed out by more than one writer as an ominous circumstance, that the event, which more than all others was taken by those who brought it about to be a triumph of ultramontane principles, coincided with another, which heralded the greatest disaster the arms of France have sustained since the fall of the First Empire. On the 18th July, 1870 the dogma of Papal infallibility was proclaimed in Rome; and on the same day the declaration of war by France against Prussia was published in Berlin.[4] "As the Pope read aloud the decree of his own infallibility," says the author

[1] *Le Présent et l'Avenir du Catholicisme en France*, 1892, p. 238.

[2] De Pressensé, writing in 1874, after giving the statistics of Jesuit institutions in France ten years previously, adds : "Cette statistique a peu d'importance depuis que l'Église elle-même est devenue une immense succursale, ou, pour mieux dire, le vaste diocèse de la Société de Jésus."—*La Liberté religieuse*, p. 96. The Jesuit colleges were closed in France in 1880.

[3] *Mémoire soumis à l'Empereur Napoléon III., sur la Restauration de l'Église Gallicane*, 1861, p. 6.

[4] Dr. J. A. Dorner, in the article before quoted, p. 591.

writing under the name of "Theodorus," "a storm which had long been gathering broke over St. Peter's; and the decree was read by the aid of a taper, and to the accompaniment of thunder and lightning."[1] It need not be set down as a mark of a weak or superstitious mind, to regard this coincidence of the two events as something more than fortuitous. Both were in fact, hastened on by the same designs. Prince Bismarck, addressing the Prussian Chamber of Deputies on December 5th, 1874, declared himself possessed of conclusive evidence to show that "the war of 1870 was the combined work of Rome and France." "I know from the very best sources," are his words, "that the Emperor Napoleon was dragged into the war very much against his will by the Jesuitical influences rampant at his Court; that he strove hard to resist these influences; that in the eleventh hour he determined to maintain peace; that he stuck to this determination for half an hour, and that he was ultimately overpowered by persons representing Rome."[2] How France suffered by her rulers yielding to the influences here spoken of, we all know. How Rome—so far as that is synonymous with the temporal power of the Pope—suffered also, was shown in its annexation by Victor Emmanuel to the kingdom of Italy, three months after the war broke out.

As the material prosperity of France has recovered in a marvellous manner from the shock, so the Church in France, as we have seen, has of late years advanced with unabated success. But whether this success is real and spiritual, or only superficial and external, remains to be proved, and the result will be watched by many with anxious interest. That there is greater discipline and subordination among the clergy is certain. But there are those who think that this result has been reached by a system of intimidation, which has crushed out the free expression of opinion on religious matters.[3] That

---

[1] *The New Reformation*, 1875, p. 90.
[2] *Ib.*, p. 91 *n*.
[3] See *L'Église Catholique-romaine en France*, par M. L'Abbé Michaud, 1875, p. 31, where the writer speaks of "l'absolutisme odieux exercé par les évêques sur le clergé inférieur." The bishops are tyrannized over in

there is a vast increase in the number of religious fraternities and sisterhoods of various kinds, is equally undeniable. But some might reply that this greater devoutness is alloyed by a corresponding increase of superstition. The Catholic religion seems to burn with an intenser flame, but the darkness outside its borders seems blacker by the contrast. To those who are content with this state of things, the system of centralization which has been going on, under Jesuit management, in France and other countries, is a "mouvement de concentration de l'Église catholique autour de son chef."[1] To others it will seem rather a persistent attempt on the part of one division of an army to make its own general commander-in-chief; an attempt in keeping with the whole policy of the advisers of Pio Nono, of those who prompted the Syllabus of 1864, as well as the Infallibility dogma of 1870.[2]

While the Church of France has thus shifted its moorings, our own has not remained stationary. The views of Archbishop Wake as to what ought to be done to restore communion between the two Churches—"to purge out of the public offices of the Church all such things as hinder a perfect communion in the service of the Church; that so, whenever any come from us to them, or from them to us, we may all join together in prayer and the Holy Sacraments with each other" (p. 77)— would now be very probably pronounced to be latitudinarian. The great object of many of our writers, since the Oxford movement of 1832, has been to show, not that anything needed to be "purged out" of our public offices, but that these

---

their turn, the Jesuits making "tous les efforts possibles pour anéantir les droits des prêtres et des évêques, pour paralyser complètement la hierarchie de l'Église de France" (p. 33). See also an article in the *Quarterly Review*, said to be by the late Bishop Wilberforce (vol. cxviii., 1865, pp. 498-529), in which evidence is produced as to the number of interdicted priests in Paris, reduced to miserable shifts, such as cab-driving, for earning a subsistence.

[1] L'Abbé de Broglie, as before, p. 15.
[2] For some strong observations on this paving the way for the final decree, by the dogma of the Immaculate Conception, see the Abbé Michaud: *Le Mouvement contemporain des Églises*, 1874, p. 5.

rather required to be stretched to a higher tension, to be kept up to their original pitch. The Church of England and the Church of Rome were as two musical instruments side by side. The strings of the former had become relaxed, and the notes they gave were flat. The instrument only needed retuning, for both to make one harmony together. "Let the inquiry be once instituted," urged one,[1] who may be taken as a representative of this spirit, "in regard to the status of the Church of England: Has she retained or lost the elements of Catholicity? Let this inquiry be made first by the Pope, and then by a council of the Church to which we willingly refer the determination of our differences. . . . True, we are separated from the visible communion of the Catholic world, but *not willingly*. We pray, we protest against such separation, and it is our comfort to know that 'it is not separation which makes schism, but the cause.' . . . Before, then, the Bishops of the Catholic Church condemn us, let them feel the heart which now beats in the Church of England. Let them judge her as to her motive—and what is that? To live and labour on in *internal* communion with all true Catholics, until such time as God will restore the *external* communion which she desires."

It must, of course, be borne in mind that such spokesmen do not by any means represent the whole of the Church of England. But they represent an active, increasing party, one from which, moreover, the appeal for reunion with the Latin and Greek communions chiefly comes. Can we safely say that between the Anglican Church, moving on these lines, and the Gallican, merged as it now is in the Roman, any close approximation is likely—more likely than it was in Wake's time? I

---

[1] See a Sermon signed "N.", on Acts vii. 1, 2, in *Sermons on the Reunion of Christendom* (First Series), 1864, pp. 159-174. The years 1864-1867 were prolific of Reunion literature. In 1867 appeared a volume of *Essays on the Reunion of Christendom*, with an Introductory Essay by Dr. Pusey. Many passages from this might be quoted in support of the statements in the text. See especially the Essay on *The Difficulties of Reunion* (pp. 88-117), by the Rev. W. Perceval Ward, Rector of Compton Valence, Dorsetshire :—"England then must be *Catholicized* before her Church can be restored to Unity" (p. 91), etc.

think he would be a bold man who should venture to predict it. We may now almost cease to speak of Gallicanism,[1] and accept it as inevitable that we have to deal with a Church dominated by the spirit of the Vatican decrees. With this, even the writers we have referred to as most desirous of a return to Catholic unity, see no prospect of reconciliation.

" It is absolute waste of time," writes Mr. Ward,[2] " to talk of Reunion, while Ultramontanism is the governing principle at Rome." If any further evidence were wanted, the remarkable letter of Pope Leo XIII. to the English people, dated Easter Day last, would be sufficient. The benevolent tone of that letter has been often and justly praised. But the serious fact remains, that in all the yearning expressed for the return of the people of this country to union with the Catholic Church, as that term is understood by the writer, there is no allusion whatever to the existing Church of England. The Bishops of that Church are silently ignored ; the rank and file of an army are addressed, without any notice taken of the officers. Nor is

---

[1] A pastoral letter of Cardinal Guibert, Archbishop of Paris, dated July 2nd, 1874, may be taken as expressive of the change thus brought about. In it he glories that it has been given to him "*se prosterner* devant Pie IX. captif et persecuté." Michaud : *L'Église Catholique-romaine*, p. 33. Compare this with the language of Cardinal Noailles, or even with that of Archbishop Darboy, in his *Dernière Heure du Concile.*

[2] *Essays*, as before, p. 107. The writer goes on to say that this "disheartening truth" has of late been brought home " in a more than usually painful way by the Pastoral Letter of Archbishop Manning." I presume that this refers to the *Charge* of Archbishop Manning reviewed with a profusion of praise in the *Dublin Review* for January, 1868. The Archbishop, who was soon to be an ardent supporter of the dogma of Infallibility at the Vatican Council, there denounces Gallicanism as "the spirit of egotism, worldliness, and avarice, which caused whole nations of Europe to apostatize from the Divine Will, from the Unity of the Church, and to erect Lutheranism, Calvinism, and Anglicanism on the schismatical basis of national churches" (p. 46). It was worthy of the same authority to pronounce that " the Protestant Reformation has reached its three-hundredth year. It has run the career which is usually permitted to a heresy."—*Essays on Religion and Literature*, 1865, p. 31. Compare, with this way of speaking of his *antiqua Mater*, the tender language of Cardinal Newman, in a passage too well known to need quoting.

there the least hint that the Papacy is disposed to make any concessions; to treat with the present leaders of the English Church as Urban VIII. would have treated with their forefathers.[1]

This mistake—for such we must consider it to be—was pointed out in a dignified manner by our own Primate in a Pastoral Letter dated from Lambeth on the 30th of August in this year.[2] At the same time the Archbishop vindicated for the English Church a position like that which his predecessor William Wake had forecast more than a century and a half before. "History," he said, "appears to be forcing upon the Anglican Communion an unsought position, an overwhelming duty, from which it has hitherto shrunk. It has no need to state or to apologize for this. Thinkers, not of its own fold, have boldly foreshadowed the obligation which must lie upon it towards the divided Churches of East and West."

I do not know whether among the "thinkers, not of its own fold," the Archbishop had specially in view Count Joseph de Maistre. But his words are so akin in their prophetic spirit, as to deserve quoting here; and with them we may fitly close: "Si jamais les chrétiens se rapprochent, comme tout les y invite, il semble que la *motion* doit partir de l'église d'Angleterre. Le presbytérianisme fut une œuvre françoise, et par conséquent une œuvre exagérée . . . Mais l'église anglicane, qui nous touche d'une main, touche de l'autre ceux que nous ne pouvons toucher. . . . Elle est très-précieuse sous d'autres respects, et peut être considérée comme un de ces intermèdes chymiques, capables de rapprocher des élémens inassociables de leur nature."[3]

---

[1] See an essay by the Rev. Frederick George Lee, in the *Essays on Reunion*, before quoted, p. 121.

[2] See the *Times*, September 6th, 1895. The Archbishop there refers to "a certain friendly advance made from a foreign Church to the people of England, without reference or regard to the Church of England."

[3] *Considérations sur la France*, 1797, p. 32.

INDEX.

Abrégé de la morale de l'Évangile, (or *Réflexions morales*), by Quesnel, 23, 35; its circulation prohibited, 36; heretical propositions in, 37.
Alexander VII., Pope, 28.
Amelot, M., a councillor, 37; envoy to the Papal court, 41.
Amersfoort, archives at, 29 *n*.
Ampère, J. J., 31 *n*.
André, Major, 5.
Andrewes, Bishop, Du Pin's opinion of, 81 *n*.
Apocryphal Books, the, Du Pin on, 112.
Arnauld, Antoine, 18; draws the distinction, *de facto* and *de jure*, 22; friend of Quesnel, 24; Racine's lines on, 24 *n*.
Arnauld, Marie Angélique, Abbess of Port Royal, 32.
Articles of the Church of England, discussed by Du Pin, 107-115.
Articles organiques, the, 123, 126.
Assembly, of French clergy, 1681-2, 11; articles of, 13-16.
Augustinus, the, of Jansen, 22.

Barbe, M., chaplain to the Dutch Embassy, 84.
Bausset, Cardinal de, 30 *n*.
Beauvoir, Osmund, 45 *n*.
Beauvoir, William, chaplain to Lord Stair, 47, 87; letters from, 48, 57, 60, 63, 64, 73, 75-76, 83, 84, 90, 93, 96, 97, 99, 100, 102; letters to, 49, 57, 65, 74, 76, 82, 83, 85, 88, 93, 103, 105.

Bissi. *See* De Bissi.
Blackburne, Archdeacon, 59.
Bologna, Concordat of, 8.
Bonaparte, Napoleon, seeks the support of the clergy, 122; his relations with Pius VII., 125-126.
Boniface VIII., Pope, 6; death of, 7.
Bordas-Demoulin, quoted, 3 *n*.
Borrajo, Mr. E. M., 107 *n*.
Bossuet, Jacques-Bénigne, Bishop of Meaux, cited, 5 *n*.; sermon of, 11; draws up the articles of 1682, 13; his *Defensio Declarationis*, 17; his *Instruction*, 20; expected to be Archbishop of Paris, 24; death of, 29.
Bourbons, restoration of the, 126, 127.
Bourges, Pragmatic sanction of, 7; repealed, 8.
Browne, Dr. Harold, on the articles, 109 *n*., and often.
Brownson's Quarterly Review, 4 *n*.

"Calot" (p. 105), "la calotte," the cardinal's hat.
Canonical institution, withheld by the Pope, 69 *n*.
Canterbury, Archbishop of, 135.
Canterbury, See of, its dignity, 83, 85.
Cas de Conscience, the, 28.
Catholic World, the, 4 *n*.
Charles X., mistaken policy of, 128.
China, missions to, 54 *n*.
Christianity, national type of, 1.
Church of England, Wake on the,

50; ordinations in the, 97; articles of the, 107-115; mediating position of, 135.
Claget, Dr. William, 45.
Clement, St., 76.
Clement IX., Pope, 22, 33.
Clement XI., Pope, 28, 41; issues the Bull *Unigenitus*, 37; issues the *Pastoralis Officii*, 62.
Clergy, state of, in France, 131, 132 *n*.
Commonitorium, the, of Du Pin, 57, 58, 98-99; Beauvoir's opinion of, 63; Wake on, 69; examined, 106.
Concordat, the, of 1516, 126.
Concordat, the, of 1801, 122; passed in the Assembly, 124.
Concordat, the, of 1813, 126.
Consecration of Bishops, in the English ordinal, 73.
Constitution, the. See *Unigenitus*, the Bull.
Constitution civile du Clergé, the, 120.
Controversy, the, with the Church of Rome, 46.
Council, national, contemplated by Louis XIV., 42; advised by Wake, 68.
Councils, general, 113.
Courayer, le Père, 105 *n*.; his library, 107 *n*.; in correspondence with Wake, 114.
Court, Antoine, writes to Wake, 92 *n*.
Cyprian, St., 71.

D'Aguesseau, Avocat-général, 21, 36; Chancellor, 62 *n*.
Darboy, Auchbishop, 134 *n*.
D'Artis, Gabriel, 76 *n*.
De Barcos, Martin, work by, 25.
De Bissi, Cardinal, 64, 90.
De Broglie, l'Abbé, 129, 132 *n*.
De Caulet, François, Bishop of Pamiers, 11.

Declarations, of 1682, the, 14-16, 44; of 1663, 16.
De Félice, G., 119 *n*.
De Girardin, Piers, account of, 47 *n*.; his oration in the Sorbonne, 52, 102; matters considered by him non-essential, 53, 61; Wake's opinion of, 75; becomes a guest at Lambeth, 105 *n*.; letters from, to Wake, 56, 61, 74, 78 *n*., 100, 104; to Beauvoir, 103; letter to, 70.
De Harlai, Archbishop of Paris, 13; death of, 24.
De Hauranne, Du Verger, Abbot of St. Cyran, 32.
De la Mothe, Claude Groteste, 97 *n*.
De Lomenie, M., 23.
De Maistre, Count Joseph, 135.
De Mesmes, Jean Antoine, 100.
De Noailles, Le Duc, 31 *n*.
De Noailles, Louis Antoine, 24; made Archbishop of Paris, 25; his character, *ib.*, 81; issues the *Instruction pastorale*, 26; made Cardinal, 27, 74; his grief at the suppression of Port Royal, 34; expels students from St. Sulpice, 35; in favour at court, 42, 48 *n*.; aware of the correspondence with Wake, 60, 63, 99; accepts the *Unigenitus* with qualifications, 104, 134 *n*.
De Pressensé, E., 130 *n*.
De Rohan, Cardinal, 63 *n*.
De Tocqueville, Alexis, 118.
De Viaixne, Dom Thierri, 27.
Dionysius, Pseudo-Areopagita, 19.
Dorner, Dr. J. A., quoted, 5 *n*., 17 *n*., 44, 130 *n*.
Droit de régale, what, 10.
Du Bois, l'Abbé, 86-7, 93, 99, 101 *n*.; Archbishop of Cambrai, and Cardinal, 105, 106.
Du Pin, Louis Ellies, a doctor of

INDEX. 139

the Sorbonne, 29; account of, 47 *n.*; works of, 49 *n.*, 52, 75 *n.*, 80 *n.*; *Commonitorium* of, 57, 115; *Relation* of, 96-8; portrait of, 93, 100; his opinion of the Pope's supremacy, 75 *n.*; of the thirty-nine articles, 107-115; his letters and papers seized, 86, 88; death of, 92-93, 99; letters from, 48, 49, 51, 78, 99 *n.*, 115, 116; letters to, 51, 66, 94.

Embassies, chapels of the, in Paris, 84, 96 *n.*
England, Church of. *See* Church.
English Chapel, in Paris, 75; services at the, 76, 85, *n.*
Eucharist, rubric relating to the, 77.
Eugénie, the Empress, 130.
Explication des Maximes des Saints, par Fénelon, 20.
Exposition de la foi catholique, the, 26, 45; first edition of, withdrawn, 45.
Exposition of the Doctrine of the Church of England, the, 45.

Fabroni, Cardinal, 42.
Félice. *See* De Félice.
Fénelon, Archbishop of Cambrai, 19; his *Explication*, 20; letter of, to his nephew, 38 *n.*; advocates the calling of a general Council, 41; death of, 41.
Fesch, Cardinal, 125.
Firmilianus, Bishop of Neo-Cæsarea, 71.
Forbes, William, Bishop of Edinburgh, 80.
Francis I., 8.
French Church, the modern, state of, 118; increased power of, 129, 131.
French Clergy, sufferings of the, 121.

Gallican liberties, set at naught by the Pope, 68-69; DuPin's estimate of, 79.
Gallicanism, what, 1, 3; dominant under Louis XIV., 3; modern ultramontane opinion of, 4; early history of, 5; charged with being Erastian, 8; revived by Napoleon I., 123; whether extinct, 134; denounced by Cardinal Manning, 134 *n.*
Gasquet, Father, 115 *n.*
Gerberon, Dom, a Jansenist, 25.
Gerson, Jean, Chancellor, 7; account of, 79 *n.*
Gray's Inn, and James II., 45.
Grégoire, le citoyen, cited, 7 *n.*, 79 *n.*
Gregory, XVI., Pope, 128.
Gualterio, Antonio F., Cardinal, 42 *n.*
Guettée, l'Abbé, quoted, 9, and often.
Guibert, Cardinal, 134 *n.*
Guyon, Madame, 20.

Harris, Dr. John, 74, 83.
Hideux, le Docteur, 102, 103.
Holland, Old Catholic Church of, 26 *n.*
Horner, (?) 96 *n.*
Hudson, S., on the Church, 2 *n.*
Huet, F., quoted, 3 *n.*

Immaculate Conception, dogma of the, 132, *n.*
Indulgences, Du Pin's opinion of, 109.
Innocent X., Pope, 22.
Innocent XI., Pope, 11, 12; Fénelon appeals to, 20.
Innocent XII., Pope, 27.

Jansen, Cornelius, 22.
Jansenists, 23 *n.*; "Calvinists saying mass," 26; numerous in the French Assembly, 120.

INDEX.

Jansen, de, Cardinal, 4 *n.*
Japan, missions to, 54 *n.*
Jervis, W. Henley, quoted, 6 *n.*, and often.
Jesuits, champions of ultramontanism, 3; enemies of Gallicanism, 9; growing feeling against, in France, 34; suppressed by Clement XIV., 127; restored by Pius VII., *ib.*; influence of, at the court of Napoleon III., 130; their colleges closed, *ib. n.*; policy of, 132.
Joly de Fleury, Guillaume François, Procureur-général, 57, 61; account of him, 62, *n.*, 63 *n.*; Wake's praise of, 72; to have a copy of Wake's letter to Du Pin, 73, 74, 86, 89, 99.
Jourdain, le Père, 23.

King, Sir Peter, on disputes about non-essentials, 81 *n.*
Kitchin, G. W., catalogue of the Wake MSS. by, 106 *n.*

La Chaise, Père, 24.
Lafiteau, Messire Pierre-François, quoted, 4, and often; his opinion of the correspondence, 87-88.
Lambert, le Docteur, 104.
Lambeth degrees, origin of, 83 *n.*
Lee, G. F., 135.
"Legatus natus," what, 83.
Leger, Dr., 63 *n.*
Le Normant, Bishop of Evreux, 64.
Leo X., Pope, 8.
Leo XIII., Pope, letter of, to the English people, 134.
Le Roy, Albert, 4 *n.*, and often.
Le Tellier, Charles-Maurice, 12 *n.*
Le Tellier, Michel (confessor to Louis XIV.), 9, 12 *n.*, 36.
Le Tellier, Michel, Chancellor of France, 12 *n.*

"Licence Courante," 101.
Liturgy, the English, in what objected to by Gallicans, 77.
Louis, Saint, 5.
Louis XIV., under Jesuit influence, 9, 42; claims the "droit de régale," 10; enforces the acceptance of the Bull *Unigenitus*, 37-40; contemplates a National Council, 42; dies, *ib.*
Louis XVIII., mistaken policy of, 127.
Lullin, M., 102, 103.

Maintenon, Madame de, 31 *n.*
Manning, Cardinal, 134 *n.*
Marculfus, Gallic monk, 115.
Martin, l'Abbé, on the French Church, 118 *n.*, 121, 125 *n.*
Maury, Cardinal, 125.
Maximes des Saints. *See* under *Explication*.
Melun, 9.
Michaud, l'Abbé, 131 *n.*, 132 *n.*, 134 *n.*
Molinos, Michael, 20.
Monasteries, state of, in France, 118.
Moutarde, E., 30 *n.*
Mysticism, finds a home in France, 19.

Napoleon I. *See* Bonaparte.
Napoleon III., 130, 131.
Newman, Cardinal, 134 *n.*
Noailles. *See* De Noailles.

Old Catholics, the, 26 *n.*
Orders, the English, 115 *n.*
Ordinations, in the English Church, 114.
Organic Articles, the. *See* Articles.
Orléans, le Duc d', Regent, 42, 99, 101.
"Oud Roomsch" church, the, 26 *n.*

INDEX.

Papal claims, resisted in England, 67; Papal infallibility, dogma of the, 130.
Pastoralis Officii, the Bull, 62, 86 *n.*; reception of, in Paris, 63; appealed against by De Noailles, 64.
Pavillon, Nicolas, Bishop of Alet, 11.
Pensées pieuses, the, 23.
Petitpied, Nicolas, account of, 29 *n.*, 99; form of religious service used by, 100.
Petitpied, of Vaubreuil, brother of the preceding, 39 *n.*
Pew-system, the, 128.
Philip le Bel, 6.
Piers, Patrick. *See* De Girardin.
Pisa, Council of, 7, 79 *n.*
Pius VI., Pope, 121; death of, 122.
Pius VII., Pope, 124; a prisoner, 125; kind feeling of, for Napoleon, 126.
Pius IX., Pope, 131, 134 *n.*
Pomponne, Le Marquis de, 33.
Pope, primacy of the, 65, 68-69, 86, 116; excessive claims for, to be proved, 69; to be resisted, 71.
Port Royal, Convent of, 31; suppressed, 33.
Pragmatic Sanction, of 1269, the, 5, 79; of Bourges, 7, 8, 79; revoked by Louis XI., 8.
Preston, Viscount, 44.
Prevost-Paradol, M., quoted, 128 *n.*, 129.
Problème ecclésiastique, the, 26; publicly burnt, 27.
Protestants, stumbling-block to, 18; severities towards, in Paris, 84; toleration for foreign, 91; relations of the English Church to, 97 *n.*
Purgatory, Du Pin's opinion concerning, 108.
Pusey, Dr. E. B., his *Eirenicon* quoted, 65 *n.*, 80, 109 *n.*, 110, 113,
114 *n.*, 115 *n.*, 116 *n.*; essay by, 133 *n.*
Puyol, l'Abbé, quoted, 3 *n.*, 5 *n.*

Quesnel, Pasquier, 23; attaches himself to Arnauld, 24; draws up the *Abrégé de la morale*, 23.
Quietism, rise of, 19.
Quinant, le Docteur, 102.

Racine, quoted, 9.
Ras de St. Maur, 87.
Réflexions morales, the, of Quesnel. *See* under *Abrégé de la morale*, etc.
Reform, "pretended," 67 *n.*
Reformation, the English, Wake's outline of, 67-68.
Regent, the. *See* Orléans, le Duc d'.
Relation, the, of Du Pin, 98.
Reunion, lectures and sermons on, 133 *n.*, 134.
Revolution, the French, 118.
Richer, Edmond, 79 *n.*
Roccaberti, Archbishop of Valentia, 17 *n.*
Rohan, Cardinal, 9, 90.
Rubric, "the black," 77 *n.*

Sacrament, definition of, 109.
Saint-Simon, *Mémoires* of, quoted, 9 *n.*, 24 *n.*
Scriptures, the Holy, sufficiency of, 111.
Sorbonne, the, proceedings of, in 1701, 28; discusses the bull *Unigenitus*, 39; violent scenes in, *ib.*, 88 *n.*, 104 *n.*; De Girardin's oration in, 52; its reception there, 61; appeals against the *Pastoralis Officii*, 64.
Stair, Lord, 65; intercedes for Protestants, 84; public entry of, into Paris, 87.
Stephanus I., Pope, 71 *n.*
Stillingfleet, Bishop, quoted, 2.
Supererogation, works of, 112-113.
Syllabus, the, 132.

Taine, Henri, on the French Church, 118, 119 *n.*, 129.
Talleyrand-Perigord, Charles Maurice de, 119.
Tellier. *See* Le Tellier.
Tenison's Library, 107 *n.*
"Theodorus," 131.
Thirlwall, Bishop, 77 *n.*
Timothée, le Père, 35, 41.
Tradition, 111.
Transubstantiation, Du Pin's opinion of, 110.
Tremoille, Cardinal, 36, 41.

Ultramontane, origin of term, 3.
Ultramontanism, language of modern, 4 ; Louis XIV. attempts to check, 16 ; increase of, 130.
Unigenitus, the bull, 35, 37 *n.* ; its reception in France, 38 ; registered in Parliament, 39 ; discussed in the Sorbonne, 39 ; amount of interest shown in, 40 ; appealed against, 48 ; objected to by the Sorbonne, 73, 101.
Union between the Gallican and Anglican Churches, Wake on, 50, 58, 77, 94, 117 ; De Girardin on, 56 ; Du Pin on, 98 ; failure of attempts for, 106 ; other writers on, 133, 134.
Urban VIII., Pope, condemns the *Augustinus*, 22, 135.

Variations of doctrine, 45.
Vaudois, the, 92.
"Veniat," what, 102 *n.*
Vialart, Félix, Bishop of Châlons, 23.
Vineam Domini, the bull, 30 ; conditionally accepted, 31.

Wake, Dr. William, Archbishop of Canterbury, early life of, 44 ; weak health of, 94 ; his translation of the *Epistles of the Apostolical Fathers*, 46 ; other works of, *ib.* ; his position in relation to dissenters, *ib.* ; his correspondence with foreign nonconformists, 47 *n.*, 91-92 ; his opinion of the dignity of his see, 58, 83, 85 ; decides to meet the advances of Du Pin and De Girardin, 65 ; papers left by, 106 *n.* ; letters from, 49, 57, 65, 66, 70, 74, 76, 82, 85, 88, 93, 94, 103, 105 ; letters to, 48, 49, 56, 57, 61, 63, 64, 73, 74, 75-76, 78, 78 *n.*, 83, 84, 90, 93, 96, 96 *n.*, 97, 99, 99 *n.*, 100, 102, 104, 115, 116.
Ward, W. Perceval, 133 *n.*, 134.
Wilberforce, S., Bishop, 132 *n.*
Wordsworth, Dr. Christopher, 128.

Xavier, St. François, 54 *n.*

ERRATA.

P. 23, line 21, *for* St Beuve, *read* Ste Beuve.

P. 42, line 3 from bottom, *for* De Tellier, *read* Le Tellier.

LIBRARY ST. MARY'S COLLEGE

www.ingramcontent.com/pod-product-compliance
Lightning Source LLC
Chambersburg PA
CBHW030338170426
43202CB00010B/1168